ELIMINA

MIND YOUR **HABITS**

The Quick and Easy Way To Remove bad Habits And Addictions, Procrastination and Negative Behavior.

Written By:
Andy Raingold

Graphic Design By: Stephen Hawkins.
Special Thanks To Nathanial Dasco & Ikhide Oshoma

Andy Raingold - ThinkeLife
Visit my website at **www.andyraingold.com**

First printing: Jan 2022.

ISBN: 978 1 913929 93 0

ELIMINATE THE NEGATIVES SERIES

MIND YOUR
HABITS

The Quick and Easy Way To Remove bad Habits And Addictions, Procrastination and Negative Behavior.

Written By:
Andy Raingold

Graphic Design By: Stephen Hawkins.
Special Thanks To Nathanial Dasco & Ikhide Oshoma

Andy Raingold - ThinkeLife
Visit my website at **www.andyraingold.com**

First printing: Jan 2022.

ISBN: 978 1 913929 44 2

Table of Contents

ELIMINATE THE NEGATIVES SERIES

DEFEAT AND DUMP **PROCRASTINATION**

The Quick and Easy Way To Remove bad Habits And Addictions, Procrastination and Negative Behavior.

Written By:
Andy Raingold

Graphic Design By: Stephen Hawkins.
Special Thanks To Nathanial Dasco & Ikhide Oshoma

Preface

What's in a book? And what's in this book? Let's begin by answering the first question. No doubt you will already know the answer but humor me as we go through this together. Although a book is made up mostly of words, words are not what is within a book. Pictures are within a book. If you are reading a novel about dragons then the book contains scenes and images of dragons as you progress through the story in an almost holographic way. With every word that you read you piece together within your mind scenes and images contained within the story. Whether it's a story of dragons or a story of romance or monsters. You form images instantaneously as the words on the page are read.

With non-fiction books, books that contain information, systems, theories, and processes, you still form images but the images are approached in a couple of different ways. First, you may imagine what the author is saying and attempt to create images in your mind of the process he is describing through his words. Or, you have advanced your mind to the degree that you can interpret what the writer is saying as it relates to your own situation. Usually related to the reason for reading the book in the first place.

At a fundamental level that is how the mind works when reading a book. But as suggested, you are already aware of this either consciously or unconsciously. In most cases this is unconscious but within this book, we want to make this process of creating images a conscious one.

So, as you read the pages to follow bear this in mind and constantly and consciously relate what is being suggested to your own circumstances. The first part of the book covers the subject of procrastination so if you suffer from this life-sucking habit then relate what these words and images are saying and what they mean to you as you discover where you procrastinate and the possible root causes. With this in mind, take plenty of notes of the ways that this relates to you and the insights about your own life that are thrown into your conscious mind via your unconscious mind.

So, now we have covered the first question, "what's in a book?" let us now cover the second question. What's in this book? Again, there are images within this book that are based on the previous answer to the question "what's in a book?" those images relate to you personally and to your current and possibly future life. It is these images that we need to make notes of as in most instances they are integrated answers from the unconscious based on all the current knowledge available and becoming available through this book as well as others you will read in the future.

In a pure word and theory-based sense, the first two parts of this book give the foundational information that gets your mind focused and ready for the third part of the book. The third part of the book is really the value of this book but without first focusing on the theory and a fundamental understanding of the first parts, the third part wouldn't be done justice. I say that because by the third part you will know what habits and addictions are keeping you from acting toward what you really want out of life. So, the first parts are intended to get the reader focused on the issues that are currently being lived.

It is this first action of gathering the information that begins the process to eliminate the negatives. In fact, the process really began when you searched for this book and then purchased it. Purchasing it reinforced your commitment. Your commitment to the choice you made to buy the book. All of this is done through your personal power to decide and choose something. It is the decision made at the core of your being followed by the actions you take that begins the process of elimination. Eliminating the negatives and bad habits easily as it were. We will come to why I say easily soon.

When you do the initial work of making notes through the first parts of the book and focusing and relating them to your own situation you are preparing the ground for a piece of knowledge, or program to be placed in your mind once accepted by your conscious mind. This adds power to your efforts as you will come to experience for yourself by the time you finish reading this book.

Of course, if the reader expects to get results without any effort, then delusion and a bad book review may follow. But, if the reader takes notes, does the work, and then follows through with the practical method no matter how foolish it may first seem, then the elimination of bad habits and addiction will be almost automatic.

The nugget of knowledge or program I am speaking of will add power to your initial thought to help you come to understand that you don't actually have any addictions at all. Whether you have been led to believe that you do or not. You don't.

Of course, I am not a qualified doctor and so if you believe that you need to seek a doctor's advice then please do that. This information is supposed to integrate with any and all other methods no matter what they are, so please do not even begin to think that I am advocating a "dump everything else and just listen to me" approach. I am not. Seek help where needed. This book is part of your help and not a substitute for it.

Saying that the solutions you seek to eliminate any and all addictions and life situations is and always has been with your own thought. The power comes from here and not from a clinic, medication, or other so-called cure for whatever addiction or bad habit you may have. But again, please seek advice from a qualified medical practitioner if you feel that you need to.

I was saying, the power comes from your thoughts and not an external source of any kind. In fact, the knowledge you are receiving this very moment is already known by your subconscious, if not by your conscious mind. But authorities of just about every kind have managed to convince people that the source of the problem is external and therefore not under your control. Nicotine is highly addictive and other such manipulations, whether true are not come to be accepted by the conscious mind and then adhered to by the subconscious, which then gives the appearance of an uncontrollable addiction. The individual then believes the source of the cure is external, with an external authority of some kind. It is not. The source of the cure is you. Your thoughts, which is why you should always Mind Your Habits.

Having said that, the power also comes from your perspective and this is what this book is intended to do. Alter or add to your current perspective. As such, this book will attempt to add a "Perspective Program" into your conscious mind which when accepted to be true begins to work for the individual on a subconscious level. This makes giving anything up that you do not want quick and easy.

As I write this, I recall the hundreds of times I have been given a so-called secret to this that or the other, when in fact there was no secret at all. However, I believe the way I present this information and that leads up to the program installation really is a secret. It's a secret you can use for anything you want to eliminate or indeed gain, but it tends to work faster on things that you want to eliminate. Maybe because you come into contact and are therefore speaking directly to your unconscious mind. Not only that, but you are in complete control of what you want to eliminate and that isn't entirely true when you want to attract or gain something. In most cases, other people have what you want which complicates things somewhat.

Of course, all of this power within your enhanced perspective must be backed by:

1. **Your desire to quit what you say you want to quit.** Whether that's a simple smoking addiction or a noisy neighbor. Or anything in-between.
2. **The belief that this method works.** This is a difficult one as beliefs generally have to be built over a long time until they begin to stick. They begin to stick when you KNOW that the belief is true through your direct experience. And again, once I reveal the secret, the perspective program, you will come to understand what's really been happening with your negatives, no matter what they are. Then you will come to see and therefore KNOW that this method will absolutely work.
3. **Your ability to do the work and then follow through** with the practical exercise.

About The Practical exercise

As I just suggested the practical exercise does not begin to work once you have tried it. The exercise begins to work the moment you decide and then choose to make use of it. Even before you have actually used it. And of course, you must then make the effort to solve a particular problem starting with the initial core thought and so from the point the thought is created the practical exercise begins to work. Even before you know what the practical exercise is. In short, you are constantly choosing the success or failure of what you are currently doing as well as what you intend to do.

Now as suggested, the exercise I give isn't completely necessary and is just a catalyst to converse with the unconscious. But saying that, paradoxically, the exercise is absolutely necessary. Simply because you have already taken the first steps in this particular direction. Only when you change your mind will the exercise not be needed and so the individual can replace it with anything he wishes. Action or inaction, this method or that method.

On the other hand, it only becomes unnecessary when you have gone through it and realized that you could have used any method. But I say this very loosely and need not have mentioned it at all. I just want to be completely transparent and inform the reader that the exercise itself may be nothing new, but the process requires that you go through it nevertheless. The exercise itself will either work for you or may introduce you to some other method along your path that will ultimately culminate in the elimination of your bad habit, addiction, or any other negative situation.

Certain tools will be required to adopt the practical method and I have provided some of them. But it is a vital part of the eliminating process to create the tools yourself. I have provided video instruction to guide you through the creation process and it's really quite simple. But more on that later, just make up your mind right now that you are going to do what is required and needed in order to quit the negatives starting with the most pressing. As for what the negatives are, it doesn't matter, you will create lists of each area as we progress in the first two parts as well as digging much deeper in the third part of the book. And as suggested, make the decision at the beginning that the process will work for you and believe in that and it will work wonders in your life. This is akin to, "There is no try, do or do not" which becomes "there is no maybe, succeed or succeed not."

As I said, the method starts to work just as soon as you make the decision to eliminate the negatives because no method really works, they are all just catalysts to get the individuals mind to work, and so, if you feel sudden urges or surges of strength and determination rise up within you as this book unfolds then act on those urges. It is your unconscious getting the message through your conscious choice and then forcing or pushing you into action, to do what needs to be done as I make suggestions and through your own urges.

I purposely avoided using the word intuition here as some people seem to believe they are not intuitive at all. That's just not true but it is also not a subject we want to get sidetracked by here. Simply act on your urges. If you get the urge to go to a stop smoking clinic, for instance, make an appointment and continue with this process. Do what you urge yourself to do as you become aware of those urges here.

Follow through and complete the process and you will soon find your addictions dissipating.

PART 1:

The Cost of Procrastination

Introduction

Have you ever wondered why you haven't achieved your life goals up to this moment? The reason for this is likely to be the kind of habits you have built over time. One bad habit that has stopped many people from actualizing their goals sooner rather than later is the habit of procrastination, and if you are here, reading this now, then I believe that procrastination is holding you back, and you want to do something about it before it's too late.

I understand that sometimes you may feel helpless at overcoming a habit that has become such a part of your life. However, the good news is that you can still defeat procrastination, achieve your goals and live the kind of life you have always wanted. And of course, my book Eliminate The Negatives can help you to eliminate other negative habits and behaviors but here we will just stick to procrastination as it is a central, or core habit that can stop you from simply acting towards any given, preplanned end.

The first part of this guide aims to emphasize just how much the habit of procrastination has cost you so that you can develop the motivation to defeat procrastination once and for all.

It also provides the most simple, actionable steps you can take to end the procrastination cycle in your life. It doesn't matter how many times you have tried to stop procrastinating and failed. What matters is that you are here, now, and that you begin to take action to eliminate the supreme negative of procrastination.

The previous book in this series as suggested will help you to remove any negative habits behaviors or situations that result in a negative life experience. And, the third book in the series titled: Freedom From Addiction goes much deeper into addictive behaviors that lock you into life half lived, and at the mercy of negative addictions. But the book you now hold in your hands will help you to remove procrastination so that you can begin to act on Eliminating The Negative Situations and behaviors, addictions, and other negative circumstances and experiences, that will then allow you to move towards greater possibilities and more positive life experiences in the future.

Chapter One: The Cost of Procrastinating

The scary thing about procrastination is that it can have very damaging effects on virtually every area of your life both in the short term and the long term. Imagine what you lose when you fail to take action on your dreams and pursue your business, career, academic, health, or relationship goals. And remember that over time growth as in many other areas of life shifts into exponential growth. But in more general terms, you can lose the love of your life when you fail to take action on time. You can lose your health when you fail to take the right steps and build healthy eating, workout, and personal hygiene habits over time. You can lose your financial independence when you fail to pursue your business dreams and other financial goals such as saving, investing, and living debt-free.

Let us take a look in more depth, at the price that you pay each time you procrastinate:

You Lose Valuable Time

Imagine how much time you have wasted throughout all of your life procrastinating. Imagine if you had made good use of your time and taken timely actions on your dreams whatever they are. Then imagine if you had built resistance against procrastination beginning earlier in your life. Life would have been a whole lot different now, and you would have become more productive with your time which would have obviously produced much better results for you to enjoy. Nevertheless, it is never too late to correct the wrongs and start making good use of your time by taking timely actions.

The worst thing that can happen to anyone who is on a mission to make something of their life is to wake up one day only to discover he has wasted five, ten, or twenty years without making any significant progress on the path they have chosen. The terrible thing about such sudden discoveries is that you can't turn back the hands of time to make those lost years count for something. And so, in some cases, regret enters the mix which then perpetuates the existing procrastination.

This is what procrastination does to you. It stops you from experiencing life in the present, makes you lose valuable years, and leaves you living in regrets for the rest of your life if you don't fight it early enough to get what you can from life... and its many experiences that could, and are still available to you.

Many people fail to achieve significant things because they do not put their time into good use and not because they have limited time or skill available to them. Most of us work 8 hours a day for five days every week, which amounts to 40 working hours a week. If we go with the recommended number of hours for sleep a day, the average adult also spends about 40 hours asleep during weekdays. If you spend 40 hours a week working and another 40 hours a week sleeping, you still have a third, 40 hours, which is more than enough to pursue your personal goals. But mot bypass this time to spend it in non-productive ways.

So, when you are neither working nor sleeping during the week, ever wondered what you do with all that time? Most times, we spend all that time doing nothing other than thinking about the things we have always wanted and why we don't have them. Imagine if you use all that free time to pursue your career, financial, business, relationship, education, health, and fitness goals? Imagine what you would achieve if you use all those free hours a week plus the weekends to pursue your personal goals, projects, and dreams.

There is no limit to what you could achieve when you put all that time into good productive use, but procrastination won't let you focus enough to notice how much time you waste on nothing.

According to a survey carried out on some 865 office workers, employees spend at least 2 hours a day procrastinating on office tasks before they get anything done. That's a whopping 10 hours a week! Imagine how much those 10 hours would have added to the average worker's job productivity. Not forgetting the possibility of promotion due to the extra work that made you stand out from the crowd.

You Lose Out on Opportunities

Imagine how many lucrative opportunities you blew because you were too reluctant to take action while the chances were still present. The career opportunities you missed, the great family you would have built with that special someone if you had taken a simple step forward, the good health you would have enjoyed if you had started working out and eating right, and so on. If it were possible to look back at how you sat back and watched precious opportunities slip through your fingers, you would most likely kick yourself.

You probably didn't know such life-changing opportunities come only once in a lifetime. While you can never get back what has gone and exists only in the past, you can prepare yourself for such opportunities that may present themselves in the future by deciding never to give procrastination any more chances to usurp your life from this present moment. Life brings such opportunities once in a while to provide you with a chance to make your life a far better experience. It would better serve you to grab such opportunities with both hands as soon as they appear as if your whole life depends on them. But it is never going to be that way unless you defeat procrastination first. Followed by making some preparations for such occasions.

It Stops You from Achieving Your Goals

Goals are essential in everyone's life because, without them, nothing will change and we would just standstill. The main reason why we set goals is that we want to change certain things about our lives. And when procrastination comes into play, achieving such goals and making the desired changes in our lives becomes almost impossible.

For example, if you have set a goal of losing weight and you never take the first steps of changing your diet and then working out, you will never achieve your ideal weight. Another example is if you want to start a business but keep pushing the idea aside each time you think of it because you feel the time is not perfect, and you will never be able to achieve your goal of building and running a successful business. Basically, procrastination makes you not take any step, and thus without taking action, you will not achieve any goal.

We as humans are goal-oriented beings, in that we always have a goal. Whether that's going to work, going to the kitchen to make another cup of coffee, or whether it's going out on the town to find our dream man or woman. We are always seeking something out through our goal-oriented minds. However, we pursue most of these goals unconsciously or automatically without actually taking the time to think about what we really want, and then setting goals in place that we can track, achieve, and experience.

It Can Destroy Your Career

Procrastination can have very far-reaching effects on your career. This is because a lot depends on how fast you act and what you achieve as the day ends. When you delay tasks, it only leads to the accumulation of more tasks and makes efficiency and timely delivery more difficult. This is parallel to what I said earlier about receiving exponential results. But most people quit before they receive the benefits of those results.

Imagine if you kept missing deadlines on projects and fail to meet your monthly targets repeatedly. What effect would that have on your career growth? It will certainly slow down your growth and probably destroy your career in the end. Or worse still, make it an average career and subsequently an average life.

It is easy to be overlooked when you are due for promotion in the workplace if you are a procrastinator. You can also, more easily get laid off as no employer loves having an employee who can't seem to get anything done on time. Even if the bad effects do not show up right away, it remains true that if you don't work on overcoming procrastination, it will stop you from succeeding and achieving more, somewhere along the way.

It Lowers Your Self-Esteem

One common reason people start to procrastinate is that they feel inadequate. Low self-esteem is one rather vicious cycle that every procrastinator goes through in life. If you think you are not good enough to pursue a particular goal or embark on a specific project, it is usually a good sign of low self-esteem. And the more you procrastinate due to this low self-esteem, the more you increase your feelings of low self-esteem and the more you procrastinate, and so on.

According to a study carried out on some 426 college students, low self-esteem contributed to academic procrastination and poor academic results. This clearly shows that we hold back when we lack sufficient self-esteem, and so we start feeling unworthy and unqualified for the success we seek. Procrastination will always eat away your self-confidence, gradually, until you have none left at all. If this sounds like you then please don't wait and expect things to change over time on their own. If you don't work on defeating procrastination, it will take away every trace of self-confidence and leave you unable to dare to dream and set goals.

It Can Affect Your Health Negatively

Mental health problems like anxiety and stress are among the major effects of procrastination. These mental health issues can lead to more severe health problems like depression and high blood pressure.

When you think about something for a long time and put it off, it will start weighing you down mentally and end up giving you too much negative stress. Imagine the stress and anxiety that comes with a situation such as postponing your project presentation until it is too late to do proper research and come up with an excellent presentation. Of course, some stress is good for you but lots of small occasions of being stressed will soon mount up to affect you exponentially as we have already suggested regarding any area of life.

This is also applicable to a situation where you put off going for regular health checks with your doctor, engaging in the general recommended physical exercises, or implementing a healthy diet change to keep your blood sugar, blood pressure, cholesterol, or weight in check. The more you procrastinate on these things, the more damage you do to your health in the short and long term.

You Lose Money

Most people do not know how much they lose to procrastination financially and otherwise. Mostly because they never take a good look at themselves and their life. Researchers have shown that people who procrastinate when making essential investments and financial decisions pay dearly with their own money. For instance, in 2002, about 40% of Americans waited until the last minute before filing their taxes. Such procrastination in filing their taxes costs people about $400 on average.

Experts also believe that people who procrastinate rarely put any money away for retirement plans, resulting in limited retirement savings and reduced retirement enjoyment. Further, as per a CNBC report in 2012, the average American employee incurs a financial loss of $10,000 a year due to procrastination.

With all of this basic, fundamental understanding of the negative effects of procrastination, let us now move on to possible reasons why people procrastinate in the first place.

Chapter Two: Why People Procrastinate

How The Fear of Success Makes People Procrastinate

So why do we procrastinate despite knowing the negative and often devastating effects on our lives that procrastination may have? In this chapter, we will focus on how the fear of success can make you procrastinate your life away.

Did you know that most of us are afraid of success? If you evaluate your life, you will find shreds of evidence that support this assertion in the way you approach your goals. So, what possible signs tell you that you are afraid of success and procrastinate due to this fear of success?

If you are a procrastinator, you may probably notice that you approach your goals slowly, reluctantly, and sometimes not at all. Imagine when you have a chance to pass a job interview, but you can't seem to get yourself to get up and go for the said interview because you fear the job will make you lose a part of your freedom when you get it. This is a fear of success at work, and it will always make you procrastinate. Whenever you hold back because of how much change achieving a particular goal will bring to your routine, the fear of possible success fuels your procrastination.

You may find yourself making very detailed plans to make your business work or make your new project succeed, but you can't seem to get tired of making these plans. For instance, you can plan to launch a product into the market and spend all the time designing your marketing strategies without making any move to design the product. The reason behind this might be that you are probably afraid of starting something you may not be able to handle when it grows big. This fear of not handling the demands for large supplies can probably hold you back and turn you into a procrastinator.

You may suddenly feel a wave of anxiety when it seems you are about to make it big, and you decide to slow down. Imagine a situation where you have been making progress as an upcoming artist, and suddenly an opportunity presents itself with the power to shoot you into the limelight fast. Suppose you skip such an opportunity such as a once-in-a-lifetime audition with industry giants and top brands. In such a case, you are undoubtedly dealing with a fear of success and will always put off making an appearance whenever such opportunities pop up. You could suddenly decide you do not want the spotlight on you.

Usually, people with the fear of success syndrome always admire others' success but will not want to be the center of all that attention themselves.

One of the biggest reasons why fearing success may make you procrastinate is because you do want to achieve your goals, but you do not want anything to change around you. You may feel that anything that can bring about any dramatic change will have to wait. This desire to keep things the way they have always been can stop you from pursuing your goals or doing anything that can make things different, sometimes in only small ways.

For example, you may want to start a business. However, starting and running a successful business might mean changing your daily routines and your social circle entirely. Change may feel scary if you want things to remain the same.

You may also fear that being successful can turn you into some kind of unfriendly person you never expected to be. Some people always have this notion that successful people are snobs and unlikeable people. If you feel becoming successful in your classwork or business may make you start showing people a colder than usual attitude, you may never want to pursue any meaningful goal. However, it helps to know that your belief about successful people could be entirely wrong and unfounded. If you know anyone who became successful and suddenly became loud or disrespectful, such a person probably had all those traits all along. We simply can't judge people based on what we see and believe to be true of them.

We have no idea how they feel or what they are experiencing at any particular time despite such notions of "first impressions count" and so on.

Just as much as fear of success can make you procrastinate, so too can fear of failure. Let us look at this in the next short chapter.

The Fear of Failure and How It Makes You Procrastinate

According to results from some productivity experts, the more anxiety you feel about the possibility of failing to reach your goals, the less likely you are to take any actions towards meeting those goals.

At some point, every one of us has experienced intense self-doubt or compared ourselves to others in our field, niche, class, community, or workplace. This is one major reason why most people never take critical first steps toward their life goals.

So, let's take a look at some of the common ways the fear of failure makes you procrastinate:

Always making excuses:

A chronic procrastinator will always have a reason for failing to deliver tasks on time. In as much as some excuses could be the real justification why you wouldn't get something important done on time, researchers have found that people who make excuses all the time don't take responsibility for their lives. They can't control their lives and take the right steps when needed to get things done. And the thing about getting used to making excuses for your failure is that it soon becomes a habit, and instead of doing something, you always find a reason not to.

These excuses are possibly because you do not feel good enough to get the tasks done and deliver the perfect results you are most likely after. And once you use the excuse technique and it seems to work for you, you are sure to always find more reasons to put off important work.

Making success seem insignificant:

When you set a goal, e.g., something you wish to achieve before the middle of the year and fail, one way to soothe yourself is to tell yourself, and everyone who knew about it, that it doesn't matter anyway. For instance, if you had planned to start a business, the fear of failure will make you tell yourself the story that you don't really have to achieve the goal you have set for yourself and thus refuse to take any more steps to make the dream happen in reality. Anything you may say to diminish its importance will suddenly seem valid and so make the goal seem unimportant for you to even try and succeed in.

The fear of failure can make you decide that you do not really need the new job and won't attend the interview after all. It can make you decide that the exam will no longer be worth it, and therefore no need to stress yourself trying to pass it. And of course, we can begin to make these kinds of excuses in any other area of our lives.

Withdrawing because you have never done something before:

The fear of failure can make you procrastinate by convincing yourself that it is useless to even try to succeed if you have never done what is required before. If it is not something in line with what you have become used to, you may always find reasons not to step into a particular situation. For instance, if you have had a 9-5 job for most of your life, you may find yourself struggling with the idea of going into business all by yourself.

Because you have never tried to own and run a business before, you may hold back or hold onto your day job instead of going into something you are not sure will succeed in the end.

This is usually because you don't want people to laugh at you for daring to try. Or, you don't want your former colleagues to see you as a motivation to hold on to their job and to tell themselves that a bird in the hand is worth a thousand in the bush.

Always having anxiety issues regarding your performance:

The fear of failure will always fill you with anxiety. The more you think about how terrible it would be when you fail on any project, the more anxious you become, and increased anxiety will always affect your performance or delivery.

You don't have to let the anxiety stop you because it is a natural part of the process. We always feel that mild anxiety before we take a huge step in life. It is natural to feel a little anxious before you start giving a speech or presentation, before writing an exam or approaching someone you have never met before, etc. It helps to know that no matter how anxious you feel about any of these things, you will always feel more confident when you take a step or action without paying any attention to the inner resistance caused by anxiety.

While the fear of failure is really like its counterpart, fear of success, you can always find ways to overcome them. The best antidote to these fears is to face them squarely, not minding the consequences. Yes, ignore your fears and do that which you have always wanted to do. Go in for that interview without fear, give that presentation like a pro, approach that stranger you have suddenly developed an interest in, write that exam that will make all the difference to your academic qualifications, start that business you have always deferred. When you start defying your fears, you will be surprised to find out that it is easier to defeat these fears in your mind and thoughts - which is where they are, and say yes to your dreams rather than to keep procrastinating them. Courage isn't the lack of fear, it's the willingness to act despite the fear and turn it into an ally instead of an enemy.

Chapter Three: Overcoming Negative Thinking to Beat Procrastination

Another reason people procrastinate, apart from the fears of success and failure, is how they think. If your thoughts always dwell on negative narratives, you can always be sure to find reasons to procrastinate and not go after your dreams. According to Dr. Ramesh Manoca, the author of '*Silence Your Mind,*' negative repetitive thoughts will always lead to procrastination. We will focus on this throughout this chapter and how you can overcome negative thinking to beat procrastination.

Identify Negative Thought Patterns and Step Back from Them

Negative thought patterns where you never seem to think that something good can happen in general cause negative emotions like depression, anxiety, fear, shame, stress, and unworthiness. The easiest way to learn to step back from these destructive negative thought patterns is to learn to identify them and possibly eliminate them altogether as described within Eliminate The Negatives.

Stepping back from your thoughts will involve seeing them as mere thoughts and not realities. It would be best to disentangle yourself from these negative thoughts and the adverse effects they have on you. Please note that I am not saying you will not have negative thoughts. Having negative thoughts is never the problem because it is normal to experience them once in a while. The problem is believing these negative thoughts and allowing them to dictate your emotions. Let's see some common negative thinking patterns that may arise and lead to procrastination and what you can do about them:

Anxious worries and thoughts

To bring my point to light, I'll quote Michel De Montaigne's words where he said, "My life has been full of terrible misfortunes that never happened."

Worry is a situation where your mind looks into an imagined future and comes up with images, scenarios, and thoughts about the many things that could go wrong. Worry will always make you expect bad things to happen to you such as your health failing you, your relationship failing, your career getting ruined, losing your job or a loved one, or spending the rest of your life broke. When you believe them, these scenarios could make you expect that nothing good will ever come to you and so all of this makes you procrastinate when it comes to going after the things you want in life. Stopping these worries in their track will help you beat this type of procrastination and allow you to live your dreams.

Self-criticism and self-beating

Are you always beating yourself up mentally for being inadequate, or do you focus on one or all of your perceived flaws and imagined weaknesses all the time? Constant negative self-talk will always reduce your self-esteem which then makes your confidence drop. Instead of seeing yourself as not being good enough for anything or dwelling on what is not going well in your life, you can choose to set higher goals and achieve them, attain higher statuses, and make winning an attitude and a point of focus.

Guilt and Regret

Thinking about the mistakes you have made in the past will always bring about negative feelings such as guilt, shame, and all forms of negativity. While there is nothing negative about thinking about your past mistakes, negativity can crop up when you spend so much time thinking about the many times you have failed and the many things you have done wrong, and then wishing things were different.

Instead of dwelling on the things you didn't do or didn’t get right in the past and the times you failed, think about the times you had when you succeeded, no matter how small the successes seemed to be at that time. Thinking more about your wins will fuel your willpower to step out of your comfort zone and take a targeted shot at success. But when you choose to think about the many weaknesses that can stop you and the times you failed in the past, you give yourself more reasons to keep procrastinating until it becomes almost too late to try and change the current situations you may find yourself in.

Using The "Name It To Tame It Technique"

One problem negative thinkers almost always seem to have is that they always try to resist these negative thoughts or push them away without really succeeding. But if results from studies are anything to go by, trying to struggle with such thoughts only amplifies them. If you pay attention, you will notice that whatever you try to resist or push away persists. However, you can get rid of these negative thoughts using practical techniques that require a more passive approach. You don't have to try to fight anything. According to Dr. Daniel Siegel, the name-it-to-tame-it method works well when you follow the steps below:

Label the thought: Once any idea goes through your mind, label it as a story. For instance, if you find yourself always thinking how you are not good enough to open that new business or start that new career, label it "the not good enough to start" story. Such thoughts are often repetitive and will keep coming back to you. Whenever you find such negative thoughts harassing you, simply say or state that the "not good enough to start" story has resurfaced. Recognizing the familiar thought and how unhelpful it is will help you let go of it faster. So, let's take a look at how we can make letting it go easier.

Open up to the world around you: The moment you recognize the already labeled thought, take note of your environment. Notice the birds in the nearby trees, the gentle sound of the breeze from the tree branches, the sensation of the sun on your skin, the sound of passing cars, and whatever else you can find around you.

Doing this can help you step away from the negative thoughts that make you procrastinate.

While naming your thoughts, ensure to name these negative thoughts and emotions soothingly or in a calm state of mind. You don't want to engage in any form of struggle or fight with the thoughts. Make them something to be laughed off to help you feel more at ease when you begin the process of focusing on your immediate environment with a calmer attitude.

Come Back to Your Senses

According to the words of James Thurber, "*Let us not look back in anger or forward in fear, but around in awareness,*" most negative thoughts will come either from past mistakes and the shame and guilt they awake within you, or worries about the future and fears of what may happen or may not happen to you, your loved ones, and the world around you. These thoughts may increase stress as you worry about your ability or inability to achieve your set goals.

What these thoughts on past mistakes and worries about the future do is that they make you lose touch with the present moment, its pleasures, and numerous wins available in the future and already experienced. You can step out of these negative thoughts about the past or future by engaging your senses to focus more attentively on the present moment.

So, how do you come back to your senses when negative thoughts try to stop you and make you procrastinate? Simply bring your attention to where you are at the moment, what you can see, smell, taste, or see. Notice the nearby flowers' scent, the taste of whatever you are eating, any sensation the weather has on your skin, etc. Research carried out by Prof. Mark Williams, an Oxford University professor, showed that it is much easier to focus on our current sensory experiences than it is to fight our negative thoughts.

How to Increase Your Focus to Overcome Procrastination

All right, let's consider a familiar scene to help you understand how increasing your focus can stop you from procrastinating.

Imagine sitting at your work desk with lots of work papers to attend to right in front of you. You are lost in daydreams about the possible vacation locations to explore on your next trip or the thoughts about how wonderful life would be when you finally get the one you admire to fall in love with you. Your head is filled with every imaginable thought except the workload before you and how to reduce it. You can spend a whole hour or more in this state without moving a finger to get any work done. You put away any thought about work from your mind and leave the workload for later because you simply lack focus.

The initial daydream can also develop roots into many and varied similar daydreams that end up stealing your life away rather than being a creative and imaginative pursuit.

Apart from having your mind filled with daydreams like these, several other factors can make you lose focus. You can get also distracted when you are tired, hungry, thirsty, or even overfed. However, you can always find a way to refocus and motivate yourself to work, irrespective of whatever is getting you distracted.

So, what steps can you take to sharpen your focus and beat procrastination? Here are some examples:

You can take a momentary leave of absence
One amazing technique you can use to stop procrastination due to lack of focus is to stop everything you are doing and do nothing on purpose for a while. When I say take a short leave of absence, I advocate for mindfulness meditation. The hustle and bustle of daily life can take its toll on your mind and body. It will do you a world of good to clear every thought from your head through meditation. And as suggested it's a more creative pursuit rather than an exercise in daydreaming for the sake of daydreaming. The outcome is that you can then move into your work focused on what needs doing.

The thing with meditation is that you do not need any religious rituals like burning some special candles or playing some recommended ambient music to get the best results from meditation. All it takes to help your mind refocus is to find a comfortable place to sit still, focus on taking some steady deep breaths, and resist dwelling on any thoughts except the thoughts of your breaths.

So, no matter how busy your life has become, find time to escape the world around you for a few minutes a few times a day to enable you to achieve mental clarity and increased focus. You will be amazed at how much you can get done after spending a few minutes clearing out mental fogs through meditation.

The Elephant-Eating Approach

The thought of embarking on large projects with many tasks will always be scary and can make you lose focus because it feels like it is too much to handle. But you can make it easier for yourself by taking one bite at a time, just like you would eat an elephant. The bit-by-bit approach helps you stay focused on each bite, one at a time, and with less interference from procrastination habits.

In general, this is the best way to tackle large projects and will allow you to overcome the temptation to procrastinate. Tackling big projects in small doses and stages makes them much more manageable and less scary. If you have read my book Success Redefined then you will already know how to eliminate any thoughts of overwhelm.

For instance, if you lack the initial focus to read a particular book and have been procrastinating because of how long the book is, you can make the task easier by setting a goal to begin by reading one page at a time. From here, move on to a chapter a day until you can read a few chapters a day successfully.

One Task at a Time

We live in a fast-paced world where everyone is trying to do a whole lot at the same time. But the fact that we are not all gifted to multi-task successfully will always leave most of us producing results that are far from being excellent. Multi-tasking can make you confused, lose focus, and leave you procrastinating on essential tasks. The conscious mind is not meant to focus on many things at the same time. So, we should avoid multitasking wherever possible.

When you take the "one task at a time" approach, you will get more done and produce the best results at the end of the day.

A good way to use this approach is using the time blocking technique. Time-blocking is a productivity hack that helps you group your daily activities into blocks. You can set up hours for different tasks and put related duties in the same blocks. Once you identify tasks that you can do together, put them in one block.

For instance, if you have to check your email and send out newsletters at work, it would be a great idea to put checking your emails and sending out newsletters in the same block.

I go into a very similar but much more powerful approach to productivity in my book titled Success Powerfunnels.

Chapter Four: Reward Yourself When You Win

Sometimes we procrastinate because we find the tasks we have to do too difficult, dull, or unexciting. No one sees it as fun to jump into difficult or monotonous tasks. Such tasks will make you lose the motivation and the willpower to stretch even a finger to get started. Nevertheless, you can stop procrastinating on such tasks by setting up a good reward system. You cannot underestimate the power of setting up a continuous reward system to help you beat procrastination over the long term.

Those juicy end-of-project rewards can become your greatest motivation to beat procrastination and start chasing your goals. But are end-of-project rewards the best approach for increased inspiration? Sometimes associating the incentives you have set for your final victory over difficult tasks may not help you beat procrastination. The aim is to beat procrastination and not push yourself to accomplish a single difficult task and still feel burnt out in the end, which will only encourage more procrastinating.

The best way to make these rewards and incentives work is to start using them earlier while focusing on any project. If you lack the motivation to start and continue during the early stages, the rewards you associate with the final wins won't make any difference. There is a need to reward yourself for those small wins and accomplishments during the early stages too.

If you can read one chapter of a book you have been putting off each day, it calls for a reward. You don't have to wait until you have finished reading the entire book before you reward yourself.

Alexander Rozental, an American psychologist, termed this as the theory of industriousness or learned intelligence. According to the psychologist, it is better to reward the process than the final result. Rewarding your progress every step of the way will help shift your focus from the final result or product to your overall performance. Rewarding your performance and efforts will help you see work as something to look forward to, which can help you to stop the habit of procrastinating.

Now that you know some of the steps you can take to overcome procrastination, you may be excited to get started and to implement what you have learned. However, before you do that, let us take a brief look at goal setting and how to set goals that will make you want to achieve them instead of procrastinating over them. We will then go deeper into procrastination in the next section of the book. But as suggested, there is nothing stopping you from taking some preliminary actions and steps based on what we have covered so far.

Setting Reachable Goals

You may feel that you are ready to overcome procrastination, and you may end up setting big goals in an effort to reduce your procrastination and achieve your goals. However, did you know that most people who procrastinate do so because they set unrealistic goals? You can learn to set realistic goals by optimizing your goals. To optimize your goals means making them as attainable as possible. According to Beth Sterne, the author of '*Put off*

procrastination put on peace,' you can optimize your goals and make them as reachable as possible. You can adopt the term "OPTIMIS" to make it easy for you to remember:

O-**Obtainable**: When you set any goal, first stop and ask yourself if the goal is something you can achieve or its mere wishful thinking. For instance, if your goal is to increase your sales as a salesman by 100%, ask yourself if you can actually achieve that within the time you have allotted for the goal. Also, ask yourself if you have all the factors available to you that will make the goal realizable. How much time can you commit to that goal daily, weekly or monthly?

P-**Precise**: Is the goal you have set precise and specific enough? It is not enough to say you will walk more every day to lose weight.

An accurate goal should sound more like, "I will walk for 1 hour every morning seven days a week". Instead of saying, "I will lose weight before the end of this month, say, "I will lose 10 pounds before the end of the month". The more precise you are about what you wish to achieve, the more reachable the goal becomes.

T-**Time Limit**: Setting a time limit on all your goals helps you stay focused on the goal. Timing your goals helps you stay motivated and take action faster. However, it is essential to make the time limit as reasonable as possible too.

To set a specific time limit, you can say something like, "I will lose 10 pounds by March 30." But make sure that the completion date you set is a realistic time frame to work within.

M-**Measurable:** What tools will you use to measure your progress? If your goal is to start working out to lose weight, you can check your weight every Saturday and put your results down in your diary. This will help you track your progress and celebrate every step of the way with the right incentives.

I-**Ink it**: You have to put the goals down on paper and how much achieving them means to you. Writing down why you wish to achieve what you have set out to achieve gives you the motivation you need to beat procrastination and get started. You may also like to write your goals five to ten times every morning to keep you focused.

You can write something like, "Reading this book will enlighten me more on the topic," "Losing weight will make me fitter and healthier." You can place the paper where you can always see it and get motivated to get up and work on it every time you see the paper. Some strategic places to put what you have written down are your kitchen sink, computer screen, bathroom mirror, etc.

S-**Share your goal**: Sharing your goals with some trusted friends, or family members can help you stay committed to the goal and celebrate the small wins as a team. When you remember the people waiting to celebrate with you when you win, you will be driven to beat procrastination and act fast on achieving the goal by not procrastinating on the "what needs to be done" tasks.

To end this section of Defeat and Dump Procrastination it is important to realize that procrastination is a monster that slays dreams if it is not dealt with decisively. Until you build up your determination not to give procrastination a chance, it will keep you at the same spot and make you live your life in wishful thinking and daydream mode at best. But with the steps and strategies in this book, you are sure to defeat procrastination and begin to live the life of your dreams.

if you know what you want out of life then you can begin to make goals and task lists to act upon just as soon as you take in all the information we have already covered and the information we will cover in the next section. So, just as soon as you are ready to eliminate procrastination and stop it from stealing any more of your life, let's move on to the next section to dig a little deeper and approach procrastination from other perspectives.

PART 2:

Defeat & Dump Procrastination

Part Two Introduction

Maybe you've heard people say "I'll get to it tomorrow," or "It can wait," or I'm not in the mood right now." If you've heard these statements or perhaps said them yourself, you are affected by procrastination. Procrastination affects a lot of people. It can drive you crazy or even upset the people around you.

Procrastination is a complex psychological behavior that affects many people. Some people only deal with it to some degree, while others have a hard time dealing with it at all. Psychologists refer to procrastination as going hand in hand with perfectionism. It is a means of avoiding some type of action or task.

People who suffer from procrastination can suffer from stress, a sense of guilt, loss of productivity, and a lot of yelling from others. If you suffer from procrastination, you know your responsibilities, but you don't want to act on them. You just don't want to commit. Procrastination can be normal if it is kept at a balance, but when you allow it to interfere in your life, it becomes a big problem.

People who suffer from ongoing, constant procrastination, after undergoing psychological tests, have been found to have a psychological or physiological disorder. In order to be able to escape from the grip of this unwelcome condition, people need to understand the whole concept of procrastination, including where it came from and why people get it.

Procrastination comes from the Latin word *procrastinatus*: *pro-* (forward) and *crastinus* (of tomorrow). The term literally means to forward action till tomorrow. This is why people, who suffer from it, always want to postpone taking action. They want to avoid the task or action and to delay it in any way they can.

Procrastination has both psychological and physiological causes.

The psychological causes can depend on the situation or specific issue the person faces. Such conditions can include anxiety, a low sense of self-worth, and a mentality where the person gives up too easily. Procrastinators have also been known to have a higher level of conscientiousness. However, this high level is based more on what they wish they can do, but they can't because their perfectionism holds them back.

Procrastination is based more on anxiety and fear than anything else. In many situations, the person simply feels out of control, and so may resort to delaying a task or avoiding it altogether.

On the physiological side, doctors have focused their attention on the prefrontal cortex. This is the area of the brain that is mainly responsible for many brain functions including planning, impulse control, and attention.

This part of the brain also acts as a filter by decreasing distracting stimuli from other parts of the brain. When this area of the brain is damaged, the person cannot stop distractions, and this leads to poor organization, loss of attention, and an increase in the ability to procrastinate.

People who suffer from procrastination are aware of what is happening. It can actually lead some people to depression or even suicide, and it can also be related to other kinds of dysfunction, such as Attention Deficit Disorder (ADD).

Although procrastination can be classed as a behavioral problem, any other symptoms that are developed around this condition can be treated with various medications. Hopefully, once the indirect conditions are treated, the resulting effect can also lessen the occurrence of procrastination. Certain medications have been known to help a person increase his attention span or even improve his overall mood.

Therapy can also be considered helpful, especially if the therapy can remove any underlying causes that created the behavior, such as fear or anxiety. The basic premise then is that it increases the person's ability to lead a normal life. This is why procrastinators should see a therapist or psychiatrist, to see if there is anything beneath the surface that is causing their problems.

Those who are diagnosed as being procrastinators could find themselves getting addicted to activities such as using their home computer a lot or using the Internet quite often. It starts with a compulsion to do something so as to avoid reality. So, they take part in some kind of activity like surfing the web or playing a video game, or other distraction.

Procrastination is like diabetes - there are different types. One is referred to as the relaxed type the other one is the tense-afraid type.

The relaxed type: views responsibilities in a negative way and avoids them by doing other kinds of tasks. An example of this is for a child to avoid doing his homework so he can play his video game. In practical terms, this is known as denial. Basically, the procrastinator does everything to avoid any situation that is not pleasurable. People who see these types think they are avoiding work but in reality, they are simply trying to evade the issue.

The tense-afraid type: is usually overwhelmed with a lot of pressure, and doesn't have a solid concept of time. They are uncertain about their goals and may even have a lot of negative feelings. This of course suggests the importance of setting goals.

They often feel they can't focus to complete their job. So, what they do is keep telling themselves they need to unwind and relax. They want to take it easy for the time being and start afresh the next day. The only problem is the next day brings the same results.

This relaxing they do eventually places more stress on them because they end up getting too close to a deadline and have to rush to get the assigned work done. Then the person feels guilty for having delayed getting it done when they had plenty of time in the first place.

Unfortunately, they repeat the same thing over and over again. They go from trying to accomplish a task to failure and delay. They constantly put off plans and goals knowing they can't complete them. The problem with this arrangement is that they can't be depended on for anything nor can they be trusted. They become uncertain about their goals and this makes them feel awkward, especially when they are around people who have it together and are goal-oriented.

Procrastinators do have a rough time of it emotionally, mentally, and even physically. But as you will learn in this section of the book, this problem can be controlled or even eliminated once you know more about the condition and how to get rid of it.

The biggest concern is to acknowledge you have it and then to take steps to change your behavior. By following certain procedures and guidelines, you may just find that procrastination can be a thing of the past.

Understanding it and getting clear as to its functions and causes will go a long way toward helping you to deal with it. It is just a matter of knowing where it originates. This is one way you can treat it. By knowing the source of the problem, you can take the correct steps to dump procrastination and then to ensure that this problem will not raise its ugly head again.

If you are one of those less fortunate to have procrastination issues, you are not alone. Did you know that even children can become procrastinators?

It is a behavior problem, usually a learned behavior.

If you find that procrastination has taken over your life, you just have to open this book and read the contents therein. Hopefully, the information in the book will then help you to overcome your procrastination habit so that you can live with yourself and know you can actually accomplish each task you start, and each goal you set.

And much more besides.

Chapter Five: What is Procrastination and How Does It Affect People?

Many people procrastinate. Procrastination in its simplest form is a behavior problem that many people suffer from. People who suffer from it sometimes do it without thinking. It can affect people's lives in a very negative and often destructive way. Some people don't even know they have the habit of procrastinating.

So again, the big question is what is procrastination?

According to psychologists, procrastination is an avoidance of doing something. People who have this condition feel that their lives are unmanageable and so they do everything possible to avoid situations just to get out of facing the responsibility of carrying out the required action. But once they're relieved to know that no action had to be taken, then they begin to suffer from guilt, inadequacy, depression, and self-doubt for failing to take the needed and appropriate action.

Unfortunately, procrastination is quite a complex psychological behavior that affects many people. Some people are not afflicted by it as bad as others. For those who are badly afflicted by it, the condition can lead to stress and anxiety.

Procrastinators are somewhat mysterious people in the way that they act. They want to take on a task right away. In fact, they are eager to do what is assigned to them. They also believe they have everything under control until they begin to do the work. Then they make all kinds of excuses for not acting and executing what they set out to do and they then react very strongly about why they didn't do it.

Procrastination is a psychological condition that has done much damage to society by slowing it down to quite a large degree.

Occasional delay in doing something is one thing. But when this attitude or behavior persists over time, it can cause many problems, including disruption in services and general workflow. Any time you decide to put off doing something it is a form of procrastination. If you have the attitude *"I'll get around to it,"* that is also known as procrastination.

If you are in business and you are around a procrastinator, you will soon know it. You will feel the effects of it. Your business will likely suffer the effects because of a slowdown in work processes and general employee tardiness. Procrastination causes problems between co-workers and the workers' relationship with the boss.

Sometimes the general morale is also affected which if ignored can spread through the company. The boss can't assign duties to the procrastinator, because he knows the work will not be done on time. In many cases, procrastinators are fired because of this.

The sad fact is that procrastination has disrupted and will continue to disrupt lives and hurt families as long as it is continued by the person who suffers from it. Those who suffer from it will continue to battle fear, resentment, anger, guilt, frustration, and other emotions, all because they can't control the after-effects of the situation and so other people get on their case because of it.

Some people, who have been witnesses to the people who suffer from procrastination, have gone so far as to believe it is a curse. That is until the situation has been sufficiently examined.

In some cases, it could be... by the way it seems to affect the person who suffers from it. But the main consideration here is the inability of the person to cope with every situation and to accomplish what they set out to do or believe they need to do.

Unfortunately, although not doing anything can place you firmly in your comfort zone, procrastination is far from being a blessing, not only for those who have it but for those who are close to the sufferer. This is where the root cause is involved. This problem causes interference in one's life and way of doing things in a very negative way. And what is worse, the sufferer knows what is happening and feels guilt or remorse for not being able to accomplish what he/she promised to do. It is as if they want to do it, but something inside them stops them from going forward and actually doing it.

It is only when procrastinators get in touch with the reality of their condition and then take steps to alleviate it, can procrastination becomes less of a burden, and maybe become a condition of the past.

Why does procrastination happen?

Suffering or having procrastination is one thing. Understanding why it actually happens is another. There really are many causes of procrastination. However, the most important point here is to first find the cause and then remove it so that the person who suffers from it won't have to suffer from it in the long term. As was stated earlier, the causes of procrastination are many. These can include the following:

Confusion and Fear: People who procrastinate often do so out of confusion and fear. At times sufferers will take on a project without knowing the outcome of their actions. When they begin the project or assignment, suddenly they get confused because the project doesn't seem to be going as well as they expected, or they were looking for different results, and therefore become confused by what the outcome should actually be. This creates fear and confusion inside them to the point where they are now uncomfortable with continuing the project.

So, they hesitate and make excuses for why they don't get it done. This fear and confusion are not based on anything real but just a mistaken notion based on some subconscious thought or reaction that they can't control. The fear aspect enters when the sufferer is confronted with the realization that such an undertaking can't be accomplished because of an inward sense of some kind of imagined doom or failure.

No Planning: What generally happens with many procrastinators is that they never make a plan of action for their projects before they start them. They just simply proceed forward with no idea of what they will do or how they will go about doing it. They just get into the groove basically, and so they believe they can accomplish the task in this fashion.

Then once they get involved with actually doing it, they come to the realization that their actions are not in harmony with the actual outcome that they seek. And overwhelm creeps in.

This, therefore, turns them into frightful, unsatisfied, guilt-ridden sufferers who now face a much grimmer reality than they first imagined. Before they got involved in the project, they should have examined every aspect of the job and what was really involved with its successful accomplishment. This way they would have known what was expected of them in order to complete the job. They would then better know what steps needed to be fulfilled in order to complete the task at hand, and how to go about getting every aspect of it done.

Of course, one mustn't forget the deadline. They must know the cutoff date for completion and keep that focused in their mind. They have to also evaluate the circumstances that would result from failure to meet the specified deadline in order to spur them on so to speak.

Lack of Analysis: One of the reasons for procrastination is the lack of analyzing a situation fully.

Every aspect of a project or situation has to be analyzed based on the results to be expected. Every part has to be examined and an estimate for the time of completion has to be attached to it. Don't try to analyze the whole event or project at once. That could very well put you into fear mode, frustration, or even overwhelm. Take what is given to you and dissect it piece by piece. This is really the only way you'll be able to work with it in a more productive and desirable way. Maybe by doing this you can deal with the whole assignment much more easily.

Lack of Prioritizing: Another reason for procrastination is the lack of prioritizing. In general, arranging tasks in a certain order helps people to accomplish them because everything is broken down and set up in regular succession. This helps to put the focus on one small task or part first, followed by the next, and the next.

When you look at a project, assignment, or whatever it is you are instructed or aim to perform, you need to list what you need to do as: very important, important, not so important, or can wait till the end to complete, in priority order.

This way you have an idea as to the most important things you need to do first, followed by what comes next, until you get to the end of the project. This way you accomplish all the tasks and don't leave anything out starting with the most important.

Avoiding Responsibilities: This is the trademark of a professional procrastinator. They hate responsibilities and avoid them at all costs. They'd rather not do anything else if they can get away with it. The main reason for this is fear of losing control. If they don't have control over the situation, they can't handle it and so give in to the pressure. This pressure leaves them feeling unfulfilled, which in turn leaves them feeling guilty for not doing what needed to be done.

Depression: Depression has long been known to be a major cause of procrastination.

The sufferer just can't get it together in general terms. The person may feel very negative, moody, and down about himself or herself. These feelings will imprison the person inside their own shell. They will not take a stand to do anything because those fears and worries have taken control. Such an occurrence is only too real for the person who suffers from procrastination.

If you approach the person and request some action to be taken for your sake or the sake of someone else, the sufferer will just excuse himself and make excuses claiming that he can't do it or doesn't want to be bothered. This presents a major problem for those involved.

Fatigue: It has been found through research that some people who suffer from procrastination have had bouts of fatigue before or during their state of procrastination.

Most of the time fatigue is based on some psychological or physical problem that first caused it. No matter, it will keep you from performing your duties, since you will not have the ability to function very well due to the fatigue.

The best way around this is to get plenty of rest and exercise on a regular basis. This will help immensely to wake the subject up and become more conscious of their actions and energy expenditure. Otherwise, the procrastinator will have yet another excuse to add to their arsenal of excuses for not wanting to perform a specific action or responsibility.

Lack of Vision: Procrastinators do not have a vision for what they are looking to do. They really don't want to go beyond the first step or two because they don't know if they will go any further simply because they cannot see any further. It is just a matter of convenience for them to stay in a more neutral position. This way there is no fear, frustration, or commitment, which makes the procrastinator feels more comfortable. Often, the mind works in layers. Only when you have completed one part of the puzzle does the second part become known.

What was covered above is only a small part of the much larger iceberg. There are many more causes that can be referenced but these are the main culprits that will allow you to recognize this problem within yourself and then resolve it.

The first thing you must do as a procrastinator is to understand why you don't want to do things that are assigned to you. Why don't you want to perform a certain task? You must analyze very carefully any project you are trying to do or are involved in, but haven't completed yet, to determine why you can't complete it. A lot of it is poor time management involved in having clear-cut goals to aim for. You may have a poor concept of time so you just think you can put off whatever you need to do to another time. If you are a good time manager, there are obviously other reasons for your problem.

These additional causes can include:

Lack of Relevance: If a project, task, or something else that you face is not really important to you, then you won't want to get involved with it as enthusiastically as if it did matter to you. You won't have the motivation to actually do it well. You will then make excuses claiming it isn't right for you or you just don't have the energy to get it done. You just don't think it is worth your time so you don't do it.

Other Goals in Mind: Oftentimes a procrastinator will be given a task to do and find that it doesn't suit them. They may not find it interesting enough so they look toward other goals to do instead. This can be a common scenario for a procrastinator. If the project is not to their liking, it won't get done.

Unless they are forced into it, the task will most likely not get done because they don't have the enthusiasm to do it, and therefore will easily quit, or just simply prolong the avoidance tactics.

Perfectionism: Perfectionism is really an ugly word but it fits into the procrastinator's arsenal perfectly. This is because, in many circumstances, a procrastinator is a person who must have things as perfect as possible in order to have them completed. This is one of many reasons why procrastinators will not engage in certain activities, simply because if they can't do it perfectly, they don't want to do it at all.

Lack of Control: One of the biggest concerns for procrastinators is not being in control. If you are a sufferer and you do something, but you find you are not in control of the outcome, you will begin to suffer from a general lack of control and will back out of the project in a hurry. You will feel embarrassed by it most probably, but your comfort zone will have been compromised to such a point that you won't be able to take the bad feelings any longer. This forces you to withdraw into a safe haven, a place where you do not have to conform, and so become an inactive participant.

Uncertainty: If you are not certain as to the outcome of an event or are uncertain as to what people expect from you, this will cause you to withdraw from it and not want to get involved at all. A certain assurance is a prerequisite to accomplishing the task at hand, and so without that there is little or no involvement at all.

Fear of the Unknown: This is a big one for procrastinators as it is one of the top reasons for procrastination. Those who suffer from procrastination do not want to get involved in any kind of pursuit, knowing they have no idea as to the outcome or what is ahead of them. They have no way of knowing how they will perform what they have to do and this leads them to not want to take the necessary steps toward action. This then puts them in a state of inactivity which can often result in depression and anxiety for fear of entrapment. And this entrapment can keep them locked in their own little world where they almost never leave.

Can't Handle a Task: If you don't feel you have adequate abilities to do a job, because of a lack of training or whatever, you may decide not to get involved or to take on the project. This has the possible outcome of keeping you in a state of confusion and disbelief. In the end, you won't partake in the task and will continue to refuse to do so. You may then use a lack of skills or qualifications as your reason for not proceeding forward.

Lack of Self-Confidence: As a procrastinator, you may have low self-esteem. You may think your effort is not worth anything so why even start? You may believe within yourself that you feel inadequate or incapable of achieving the goal of doing something unless you can do it perfectly.

I'm Busy: A procrastinator may use the excuse that he is too busy to take on any more assignments or projects, when in fact he isn't busy at all. He may even use this as an excuse if he is late getting a project done on time.

Being Stubborn: Believe it or not, procrastinators have often used general stubbornness as a way to get out of doing something they don't want to do or which they don't like. They may then go on to tell you that they will do it when they feel like it.

Manipulation: A procrastinator may use manipulation as a way to control a situation or others. They have the general attitude that no one can do a thing until they arrive, which halts the project.

Pressure Reliever: Many people will use procrastination as a way to control their lives and what is happening around them. This way they avoid pressures and anxieties that life can often bring.

Victim Attitude: Those who are procrastinators often feel like they are victims if the procrastination goes on for long enough. They can't really figure out why they can't seem to achieve anything in their life and they begin to blame outside circumstances and others.

Based on the evidence stated above, you will most likely be able to see what causes procrastination. But how do you then come to know if you really are a procrastinator? There are a number of ways to find out whether you are a procrastinator or not. If you fit into any of the following situations, you are most likely a great procrastinator:

- Do you believe that if you ignore doing a task, it will go away? For example, if you have a mid-term exam coming up, do you ignore it thinking it will disappear, although you know it won't?

- When you are assigned a task, do you underestimate it? Or do you find you overestimate your own abilities and find you can't cut it after all? An example of this would be if you undertake a test and say you find it easy and can do the test in 10 minutes when in fact, it takes you two hours to do it?

- Do you believe that a lower score on a test will still be enough to pass it? For example, you're in a math class taking a test. The goal is to get 100% but no less than 70% to pass. You believe that if you score a 68% or lower you will still pass. Because of your thinking, you lessen the effort you would normally make to do well on the test, although you realize this could lower your overall grade point average. Whether you know this or not, by committing to this pattern, you will find your life will be unmanageable and you will meet failure after failure for most of your life.

- Do you substitute one activity for another lesser activity; despite the fact that the first activity will give you better or higher results? For instance, you are told you have to complete a writing assignment that is due on Friday, but instead of working on it, you take the time to clean the house or go see a movie.

- Do you find yourself constantly delaying a project or some minor event? And do you believe that doing this is harmless? What if you have an important project to finish, but you'd rather do something else, thinking you will only spend five or ten minutes doing something else and then return to do what was required? The only problem is you never go back to the important project, and so it never gets done, or you have to rush to do it at the last minute.

- Do you make it look like you plan to do something when in fact you don't? An example would be that you promise to work on a task that has a deadline, but you have to go out of town for an emergency, so you take your laptop with you so you can work on the project while away. The only problem is you never do the work on the laptop. In fact, you keep the laptop in your travel bag tucked away in the closet of the room you are staying in.

- Do you find you are doing something but you are persevering only on one part of the task but not finishing the rest of it? A good example of this would be if you have a term paper due but you only focus on getting the introduction right, while ignoring the rest of the paper, or putting much less into the rest of the paper.

- When you are given a choice between two different projects to work on, but you are having trouble deciding which one to take. In fact, you waste more time trying to decide that, and by the time you do choose, the deadline has already passed and you missed your deadline.

If you agree that one of all the above scenarios fits you to a tee, guess what? You are a procrastinator. The way to cure yourself of the problem is by first admitting you do have a problem, and then you can take the steps to cure your problem. Once you get past the denial phase, the actual steps you need to take next are the action phase, where you get into the steps to treat the problem.

Hopefully, by the time you finish the action phase, you will no longer have to deal with procrastination. The treatment may be from a psychological perspective or it could be medical. Whatever treatment option is found, it may turn into a longer-term treatment, if your condition is worse than the standard case.

In order to really overcome procrastination, you have to get rid of many types of emotions and feelings or at least change the way you think. An example of this would be the following:

- **Difficult**: You can't sit there and think everything is difficult to do. If you do think things are difficult, you won't want to deal with them at all.

- **Time-consuming**: If you think what you will need to do will take up too much time, then this will be a defeatist attitude to adopt.

- **Lack of skills**: One reason for not wanting to do something is because the person's skill level is not high enough. This will force the person to think twice about taking on any kind of assignment.

- **Fears**: If the person has any kind of fear, this will prevent him from doing anything. He will prefer to do nothing and stay out of harm's way, rather than risk getting hurt or disappointed.

Procrastination does not have to control your life if you don't let it. If you have dealt with it for a long time, it may be harder to break free from it, but it is still not impossible. The important consideration is learning the different ways to deal with it. Then once you know them, you can take the next step to overcome the problem.

Before you can safely rid yourself of the procrastination problem, you must first recognize it as a problem. Once you recognize it as a problem, you have to come to terms with it and understand why it may be hard to get rid of.

Not all people have been cured of procrastination, at least not right away. It may sometimes take days, weeks, or even months before the sufferer can escape its evil clutches altogether.

However, once you do understand the main, common reasons behind procrastination and why it can be such a hard problem to get rid of, you can get to the root of it, and find the one ingredient that will help remove it from your own system of living for good.

The next chapter will discuss the reasons why procrastination won't go away so easily. Hopefully, after you have had a chance to read it, you'll be better able to deal with this problem within yourself and your own life once and for all.

Chapter Six: Why procrastination is a problem

As you know from reading this book, procrastination is a problem for many people, and it has affected them in many and varying ways. The causes are many and can also vary between one person and another. It really is hard to give any concrete reasoning behind the problem because each person who suffers from procrastination does so in a variety of ways. But the bottom line is that procrastination is a hard problem to solve and it seems that it won't go away easily. At least this is the way the sufferer feels about it.

1. Why won't procrastination go away?
2. Why does it rear its ugly head constantly?
3. Why can't people just get rid of it quickly so they can lead normal and better lives?

These are all good questions and the answers may surprise you. Procrastination has deep causes, which is why people can't seem to get rid of it as easily as they may want to. Although people may have made some attempt to do something about it, unless the core or root is addressed and resolved, the problem will continue onward for as long as the root is still in place.

As for the root causes themselves, there are many possibilities but here are the most common ones:

Disorganization: Whether you wish to accept this or not, general disorganization and procrastination go hand-in-hand. People who are bad organizers are usually procrastinators.

There are four levels of disorganization you need to consider since not all levels are the same or cause procrastination. These four levels include:

1. **Not being able to distinguish between urgency and priority** - Procrastinators have a difficult time distinguishing whether a problem or task is an urgent one when it must be fulfilled, and in what order it must be approached. Procrastinators prefer to

work with tasks that are more comfortable for them personally and so put off the inconvenient or troublesome ones till later.

In other words, they'd rather do what is convenient than what is urgent or what is a priority.

When procrastinators start working on the simple tasks, they find that the more urgent tasks are piling up and not getting done. Next thing they know, people start hounding them about the other tasks, so they start taking on other tasks just to quiet the crowd, but in the process, they find they get overwhelmed so they drop the previous task to take on the new task, which in turn leaves the previous task unfinished.

But at least the present task has now become a priority where it was urgent before.

Now, all the tasks that were assigned have gotten mixed up regarding execution time. Those that take on priority or urgency status are left behind for those that are more comfortable or non-urgent. Once a procrastinator gets into this situation, they are unable to establish proper priorities. This causes the procrastinator to request a reprieve from the tasks at hand and then he focuses on just the ones that are not so urgent or even have a priority attached to them.

2. **Distractions** - The procrastinator can easily get distracted to the point where tasks that may have been important are tossed aside for less important ones, mainly because they may be easier to handle or have less stress involved. If someone asked them why they didn't get the present task done they will most often claim something else came up.

3. **Being forgetful** - Oftentimes a procrastinator will simply forget what they are supposed to do. When they take on a job or a bunch of tasks at once, they may claim to have a great memory so they can remember everything. But when it comes down to it, they may still say they remember what to do by claiming they were about to do it. If you ever checked out a procrastinator's

home or belongings, you may just find they have a bunch of reminders tucked away somewhere, either in their pockets or in their desk drawers.

4. **Lumping together** - This is what procrastinators do very often. They take a bunch of activities and bring them together under one task and try to do them at the same time. When they do this, they feel they have to hurry to get everything done on time. When this occurs, they put off doing it for the reason that it is too complicated a task.

Fear: Fear was covered in a previous chapter as a cause, but it is worth mentioning here again because fear also is a common problem with procrastinators. Fear is what motivates them not to do something. Fear forces them not to engage in a task or problem and instead avoid it as much as possible. Fear then keeps the procrastination habit around and allows it to haunt the sufferer. The procrastinator struggles with fear on four levels: *rational, irrational, discipline,* or *discomfort.*

Based on these four levels they look at things from completely different perspectives, like knowing they should do it but for some reason, they just can't get into doing it, and they don't know why that is. Or, they planned to do it, but just didn't feel like doing it.

Perfectionism: This is another trait that was covered previously as a cause. But because it is a predominant trait that causes the condition to stick around, it is also covered again here.

Procrastinators can't seem to do anything unless they can do it perfectly. It has to be just right or they don't want to do it. Despite the fact they have this attitude, they will not acknowledge that they are perfectionists. They will deny this claim emphatically. Yet, they will start a project and stop it at some point, if they feel it isn't being done right.

They will start up again when they believe they are a little more in control and will continue until they lose control again. When they sense everyone around them is irritated with them, they stop what they are doing, claiming to be exhausted from what they did.

If you are not quite sure what perfectionism actually is or know of a procrastinator who does it but you aren't too sure if what they do is perfectionism, here are some guidelines that will help you determine if perfectionism is involved:

Being rigid or inflexible when doing a task.

Procrastinators who are perfectionists tend to be rigid in the way they do things. They have to make sure it is just right or else they won't comply.

Procrastinators who are perfectionists will observe a project or task is done and believe it is not being done right. Therefore, they will step in and take over even if they don't finish it.

They will have the attitude that if you give them a task to do, they will refuse to do it unless they can do it perfectly, no matter how simple the task may be.

The procrastinator who has signs of being a perfectionist will feel inadequate and will want to find closure. They will feel agitated in some way or even have some level of discomfort, if a task or assignment they were assigned to or view, is not completed. These feelings will keep that person from performing the task at hand.

Reviewing the material previously mentioned will give you some ideas as to why it is hard to get rid of procrastination. As long as the person who suffers from it has inward fear, feelings of needing to be in control, or is guided by the belief that what is done has to be perfect, they will continue to suffer from procrastination.

The person's inner self is what initially causes the problem of procrastination and it is also what allows it to continue affecting and bombarding the sufferer with continued bouts of feelings that surround the condition.

Procrastination can be dealt with and those who suffer from it can be free of it. But in order to take action and to do something to keep procrastination from becoming a major persistent problem, changes must be made on the inside first. Once these changes are made, any kind of problem that may have surfaced previously will be eliminated.

Many procrastinators just make excuses for themselves claiming they may just be inherently lazy or have other justifications as to why they behave as they do.

They put on this mask as it were, with the hope that people will understand their feelings and then leave them alone. The only problem with this logic is it doesn't work. People will be more concerned than ever and will try to pry into their lives and offer help or try to find the reasons for their behavior.

Procrastination does not have to be the dominant factor here. Instead, it can be a less dominant factor in your personality, but it takes time and a lot of effort to eventually curb its influence.

Selective Procrastination

If you suffer from procrastination on an ongoing basis, you may not do so in every area of your life. Some people procrastinate in one area and not in another. There are really five areas of life that you face daily. You may be a procrastinator in one area but not another. Or you may be a procrastinator in more than one area. It is rare that a person who suffers from procrastination is affected in every area of their lives, although there have been some who have done so.

The five areas of your life that are affected to some degree by procrastination include your *personal, school, work, home,* and *relationships*. To determine which area, you procrastinate in you have to examine many characteristics of those areas. This way you can determine the area that needs the most attention.

Listed below are the most common characteristics you will find that are associated with each area as noted above. These areas are again *personal, school, work, home,* and *relationships*.

1. **Personal**: There are many facets of your personal life that can be affected by procrastination. Let's take each one in turn:

   Eating habits - Does procrastination interfere with the way you eat? Do you delay eating because you aren't sure what you wish to eat, or don't feel like preparing a meal?

   Finances - What about your finances? Do you keep up to date with your checkbook, or do you delay in getting it done? Do you find you are behind in your bills? Always knowing where your money goes is vital to a balanced life. Without knowing this you could be in for financial disaster at some point.

   Sleep - What about sleep? We all need sleep. But are you afraid to get enough sleep because you may miss out on something, although you can't accomplish the task anyway? Does this attitude cause you to be tired all the time because of a general lack of sleep?

Healthcare - What about your health? Do you refrain from going to the doctor to get a check-up because you are afraid the doctor might find something wrong? Do you suffer from some illness or disease but you can't see the doctor because you are afraid of seeing one? Having this kind of fear can even put your life in jeopardy.

Exercise - How are you with exercise? Do you try to exercise at least three times a week or do you make the excuse you are too busy and keep putting it off? Do you have a schedule you should follow but don't because you feel overwhelmed with everything you need to do? It is important to work out 3-5 days a week. It strengthens and keeps your metabolism as well as your muscles strong and helps condition your heart and lungs. By not doing it, you can become lethargic, weak, and generally unproductive.

Personal Hygiene - What about your body? Do you keep it clean? Do you keep your hair cut to a certain length so it doesn't look long and shabby? If you are a man, do you keep your face shaved, or at least keep your mustache and beard trimmed?

If you are a woman, do you keep your hair clean and neat?
If you are to be respected by others you must keep your general overall appearance clean and respectable.

Unfortunately, some procrastinators go around dirty and even have unpleasant body odor because they claim not to have enough time to wash. Does that sound like you?

2. **School**: School is another area where procrastination can be present. This can include many different situations. These situations are usually:

   Getting to class on time - Do you find this is a major problem? Procrastinators are often late for class. Just when it gets close to class time, they look at the clock and claim they have plenty of time to get there. They then delay by doing other activities.

When they finally make the effort to get there, the class is over. Do you go through this constantly? If so, is this why you refuse to even go to college or to pursue further education? This can have a bad effect on your future life. And the problem here is that it happens to many procrastinators.

Doing homework - How do you feel about doing homework? Do you drag it out, hoping the homework will just do itself or will just miraculously go away?

Do you see your grades failing because you just can't get into gear to do it, and so you either don't turn your homework in on time, produce low-quality work, or you are always late?

Doing assigned projects - What happens to you when you are assigned projects in school? If you are teamed with other members, do you jump in and do the project because you find others aren't doing their part right? Or do you just give excuses why you can't be in the group and request to either do the work alone or with someone else?

Procrastinators have been known to do this in school and this causes more problems than it is worth. This is why the teacher will be selective in giving a student who the teacher knows is a procrastinator, any kind of project because of the way the procrastinator handles it.

Research - What about research for your homework or assignments? Do you engage in research? Do you go to your school library and do the proper research you need to get your work done? Or do you shy away from the responsibility, claiming you'll get to it the next day and find it didn't get done or you were late in doing it?

Test-Taking - How are you regarding taking tests? Many procrastinators will look at a future test as happening far in the future and will not be too concerned about studying for it until it is too late.

Then they fail the test and wonder why.

3. **Work**: The workplace is another area where procrastination can cause many problems for the sufferer. Here are some of the general areas in the workplace where procrastination can cause the most problems:

   Getting to work on time - There are too many procrastinators who lose their jobs because of chronic lateness. Nearly every day they are late by 5, 10, 15 minutes, or even more. Many procrastinators can't hold down a job because they have these lateness issues. Until they get psychological help, they just don't have the ability to find or keep a job through good timekeeping which to the employer displays a lack of interest in the job.

   Completing tasks at work - For those procrastinators who have no problem with getting to work on time, they just can't seem to accomplish a task on time. They are constantly yelled at by their boss for failing to meet deadlines. This has often caused a problem for the department the procrastinator works in because the manager has to work around this issue by assigning the task to another worker, which delays the process and production.

The boss may not fire the person but will reprimand them, hoping the problem will go away.

4. **Home**: If any place causes the most problems other than the workplace, it is the home environment. This is because when the procrastinator is at home, that person's family is exposed. This can eventually lead to a lot of frustration and confusion on the part of the members of the family. If the procrastinator lives alone, the only damage that is done is to themselves. Here are some common problems that a procrastinator may face in the home.

   Getting things repaired - If any appliance were to break down, this could disrupt the whole household. What if the TV died? Everybody would be without a TV for a while because the procrastinator would not take the time to call for service, unless, for the procrastinator who has a family, another family member kicks in and does the calling. But this could cause resentment on behalf of the family member against the procrastinator.

   Shopping for groceries - Whether the procrastinator has a family or lives alone, the one main aspect of everyone's life is to eat. How do you eat? You have to buy groceries. This is where going shopping comes in. But the procrastinator will hesitate to go shopping. The person's excuse will be that there is always time to go shopping, or they do not feel like going today. There is always an excuse. In cases like this, the person has to be really motivated to go, or someone would eventually have to force them to go shopping.

   Cleaning the house - Here is another major concern for all procrastinators in and around the home. If you go to the house of a procrastinator, you may find the house dirty, disorganized, dishes unwashed, dishes left on furniture, food left everywhere, etc.

   Some procrastinators aren't affected in this area, so this is no problem for them. But for those affected, it can be a really embarrassing problem at times which would then affect the procrastinators' self-esteem.

Laundry - What about the laundry? Does it get done? Or does the procrastinator wear unclean clothes every day? If the procrastinator has a family, someone else may do the wash, seeing that the procrastinator does not do it themselves. But if the procrastinator lives alone, do they live in a house with dirty laundry lying around? Or, maybe they manage to do the laundry but just do not put it away in an organized way. These are all serious issues the procrastinator has to deal with.

5. **Relationships**: This has got to be the most difficult part for a procrastinator to face during their life. The hardest thing to deal with as a procrastinator is a relationship.

Relationships are hard enough to gain, maintain, and then deal with, without the added complication of procrastination.

Here are some things that a procrastinator has to deal with in relationships:

Dealing with friends - How are you with friends? Can you talk to them? Or do you put off dealing with them for some reason or another? If your friend acts a certain way against you, do you take it out on the person, or do you just shy away without reacting? Procrastinators will not even move against the person, thinking that they don't want to get involved in a fight instead of facing the issue.

Going on a date - If you are a procrastinator, how do you handle a date? Do you go out with the person hoping to have a good time or do you dismiss it and hope the night ends soon? Or do you use an excuse and not go out at all? Many procrastinators feel very timid about being out in public with someone else for fear they may disappoint them and their date may not end up liking them. So, they avoid the situation by not going out at all. If this is a problem for a procrastinator, the sufferer could already be or end up very lonely.

Getting out of a relationship - If you are a procrastinator and you happen to have gotten into a relationship, but have found that the relationship has gone sour for one reason or another, you may avoid getting out of the relationship because of your feelings toward the person. Even if the relationship is bad, your feelings of low self-esteem may keep you in it no matter what has happened. This creates a big problem for the procrastinator and the family, especially if there are children involved.

If you are a procrastinator and you find that one or more of the above situations concerns you, you are not alone. There are many people who have the same issues.

Despite the fact procrastination can be a problem for people, it can at times be an advantage. For instance, the procrastinator may use his condition to delay making a decision so as to give the matter careful consideration. You can also use it to put off doing a task you may find contradicts your beliefs, which may prove to be unethical or immoral, or just does not fit your lifestyle.

Procrastination is a problem that just won't go away, or at least the procrastinator finds it hard to overcome the condition. But there is hope. In the next chapter, you will learn ways to begin to control and eventually defeat and dump procrastination.

Chapter Seven: Dealing with procrastination

If you admit that you have the condition of procrastination, within one or more areas of your life, you have made a good start toward finding a way to cure it. There are many ways to deal with your procrastination. It just takes acceptance of the fact you are a procrastinator to get you started. After all, you can't begin to cure something that you don't admit you have.

After you have accepted the fact, you are a procrastinator, there are ways you can deal with procrastination. These ways include:

Take stock of the way you make decisions. If you take too much time making decisions because you are afraid to try, wanting it to be perfect, perhaps you need to look deep inside yourself to see why you feel that way. You may want to take on the assignment, but take it one step at a time instead of looking at the whole assignment at once. This way you won't get bogged down or overwhelmed with what you are facing. The procrastinators who tried this claimed that it worked.

When you do a project, break it down into manageable steps, have a specific time frame set for each part, and focus on completing that part for that time allotted. Make sure this allotted time is within your scope or abilities to get it done. You wouldn't want to underestimate the time and find you are under pressure to get it done.

Try to plan your activities throughout the day so you can give yourself time for relaxation. This is important because if you work too much, you will burn yourself out. Not only that but if you reward yourself with relaxation time, you are in fact giving yourself credit for some desired and deserved time out. This will help prevent you from having any resentment over the chore you have to undertake.

Any time you take on a task, monitor your steps closely. Take small steps and watch for any distractions that can occur. When a problem occurs, or you have a feeling about something, handle it immediately. Don't put it off. Your feelings may be founded on real issues or they may not be. The important point is to face your fears head-on and understand why they happen.

Then take the proper steps to correct them.

If you are a perfectionist, try to remember that nothing is ever really perfect, no matter what. Therefore, go into a task with one goal in mind - to do your best and complete the task in the time allotted for the task. All the time knowing that it doesn't have to be done perfectly. It just needs to be done.

Do not put a lot of expectations on yourself except to complete the task at hand in the time frame you set for yourself. This will help you to overcome the condition of perfectionism.

Besides the above methods, you also have to take other steps so you can overcome certain characteristics that prevent you from living a fruitful life. One point of reference is to look at any fear you may have and try to understand why you have it. You have to understand the fear, identify what it is, why it is present, and then learn how to overcome it.

The best way to describe this is with an example. Let's say that you were looking for a job and you keep getting rejected over and over again.

Because of this, you decide not to pursue finding another job. Why did you decide to stop searching, just because you were rejected? Perhaps the reason you were rejected was that you kept going after jobs that did not fit your personal skill level or your qualifications. Perhaps you did not perform at the job interview very well. Examine these areas honestly.

Maybe your resume wasn't written correctly. There are so many variables to consider. The one thing you have to realize is that rejection does not mean you have to take it as an absolute. Rejection does not mean that you should take things personally. If you are not sure, you need to speak to a counselor who can examine your resume and provide a critique on your job search and interview skills, to then determine where you are lacking. By seeking a counselor, you stand a better chance of getting good results with your job search, simply because you are showing an interest which may then begin to open doors for you.

If you have problems with meeting appointments on time, try to plan your day earlier. Get up sooner in the morning so you have plenty of time to prepare. Then leave at least an hour before your scheduled time, this way you can overcome any obstacles that may come your way as you seek to get to your destination. It is also a good idea to get a calendar so you can mark your job and other appointments down.

This way you can see your appointments at a glance. It would be good to have an appointment book to take with you when you leave home so you can keep track of your appointments. Having reminders in front of you all the time will help you in your efforts to improve making appointments on time.

In other words, break down what you did during the job-seeking efforts and try to improve on each. Write down the steps for each part and then look to see where you can make improvements, whether this is in traveling to the interview, dressings for the interview, what you say at the interview, your skill levels, and abilities, and so on.

To discover your procrastination areas, break everything down like this to discover your strengths and weaknesses and do a little each day to correct your weaknesses and take advantage of your inbuilt strengths.

Other considerations and strategies to consider once you are aware of your selective procrastination areas may include these simple strategies to help overcome procrastination:

When you make plans, plan a week ahead of time. Do not go beyond that, otherwise, you may overburden yourself and start panicking. After you have completed one week, plan for the next week. Keep doing this each week for as long as you need to.

When it comes to doing any task, do not take on the whole thing at once. Instead, break the task down into smaller, related, and meaningful chucks. This way you won't get overwhelmed with so much to do all at the same time. You will only have the small, individual tasks to look at and this will help you get the job done faster and much easier. Then, when you have completed the first task, proceed to the next task.

Keep doing this each and every time you complete the task and you will find the whole project will get completed without your backing out of it.

You'll be amazed at what you did when you look back and see what you have accomplished. Remember to break down each task into smaller tasks until you become comfortable enough that you can do a task without breaking it down more.

You can take a look at the **Success Powerfunnels goals-setting website** to assist you set goals but remember not to plan too much or set hundreds of goals in the beginning, just so you can start moving into a better life situation as you slowly eliminate and dump your procrastination.

One of the most important considerations for you to think about regarding procrastination is that you have to recognize all self-defeating problems such as fear, anxiety, inability to concentrate, bad time management, being indecisive, and perfectionism. In other words, all of your negative behaviors. You can even take your first steps that begin the process of eliminating those negatives through the Eliminate the Negatives book.

You also have to identify and write down your goals for whatever you choose to do. If it is a task that you have been assigned to do, then write down your goals on paper and keep track of what you do. Do the same thing with regards to your strengths, weaknesses, values, and priorities. You must record everything. This way you can refer to it every day, which will help you tremendously in both the short and long term.

When you look at your values, you will know what you believe and what you don't. You will understand who your true self really is and where you stand on many issues you are confronted with each day.

Priorities help you to keep organized. Putting all of your priorities down in the order they need to get done and looking at that list frequently as you work, will help you immensely to overcome your anxiety of not getting the work done. It is like going to the store with a shopping list. As you shop for what you want, you see the item and place it in your cart. Then you check that item off your list. You then move on to the second item on the list and by adopting this strategy you actually get things done.

This is exactly what you do with your priorities. You simply write them down and proceed to take them on one at a time. As you complete the task, you check it off.

This really is a great way to make sure everything gets done, and you'll be surprised by how you managed to complete each task in a timely fashion. And by how much you can actually get done.

When you perform a task, look at your values, and decide if they are compatible. If so, go on and do the task. But if the task is not compatible with your values, don't get involved. Nine times out of ten, if you take on a job, task, or assignment, and your values don't match with that job, task, or assignment, you will not complete it. You will then go back to square one again and feel inadequate.

Match your values with the action or actions you plan to take.

Another factor is that procrastinators fail to utilize the concept of time well. Many of them are big time-wasters.

Don't be a time-waster. Instead, be a time manager. If you learn to manage your time wisely, you will find that all the things you used to complain about not being able to get done, because you had no time for it, will now get done because you do have time for it. You then will become elated by the time you have spent accomplishing your goals and projects and you'll begin wondering why you waited so long to do this.

The whole idea of setting goals, prioritizing your projects and tasks, and then managing your time in order to complete and achieve your goals can be transferred into the classroom too. For instance:

If you are studying in school, there is a way to easily get around your procrastination. When you begin to study, do so in small increments instead of looking at the whole assignment at once. Take a certain amount of time and study for that time. Then stop, take a break, then start the next block. Do the same until you complete the entire assignment. This will make the effort much less demanding for you.

After you have completed each short block, reward yourself for having completed that by taking a short break and then enjoying your favorite drink or snack.

You deserve it because you made it through that first section. When you take your breaks don't spend too much time on them. You'll get spoiled and won't want to go back to your work. So, try to keep them around 5-10 minutes, no longer if possible.

When you do study, have one goal in your mind, to learn and to prepare for the ultimate success - passing the test for this subject.

Try to motivate yourself to study so you can achieve this end result. The more you picture the end result of an A on your test, the more motivated you will get.

Another method you can use as you study, and many students who were procrastinators found this to be very helpful, is to create a list of sections you have to study. Maybe break things down by chapter subheadings. This way as you complete each subheading, you mark it down on your list.

By following these very simple guidelines, you will get through your homework without once giving up or postponing the task.

The most important consideration for you is to set realistic goals for yourself. This means writing down what you expect to achieve for the day, week, month, or year, and doing everything possible to accomplish those goals. Be realistic with your goals. Do not put too much on yourself at once. Instead, strive for something reachable at first. Once you have reached for and obtained that goal, shoot for the next one but start with small goals that you can reach and move on to bigger goals. Again, this is really very much like prioritizing the smaller goals that will end up supporting the larger goals over the long term.

Keep doing this in a methodical manner until you have reached all of your goals. Once you have reached all your goals, you can think about newer more distant goals. But the new goals should be higher or need more work to be obtained.

As you then seek higher goals and reach them, you'll gain more confidence and believe strongly that you'll be able to reach any goals you need or want to make. It is just a matter of believing in yourself, building that belief through progressive goals and belief in what you can do will grow.

After accomplishing many goals in your life, you will have reached heights you probably never reached before. That's right, a world of opportunity that wasn't there before will now be open to you. You'll find yourself presented with endless possibilities that will take you places you've never been to before. The secret is to start small and build over time and then not get distracted.

The main problem procrastinators claim they face is distractions in their environment. These distractions come in many forms. In order for you to handle what comes up in your life, you must remove distractions whatever they may be. Here are some simple examples within the study or education area.

Make sure you have plenty of light when studying. This way you don't have to strain to see. When you do study, don't get too comfortable, or else you will find yourself falling asleep, or not wanting to study. Make sure to sit in a desk chair or some kind of firm chair. A straight-back chair is great. This will keep you from being too relaxed. This way you can stay focused on what is in front of you, and so on.

Each area of your life will have its own challenges and possible distractions, and so it is up to you to discover what they are, make notes of them and counter them with things that keep you focused on the task at hand.

One other problem that also must be addressed here is sleep. Ever since we were children, we have been told that we need eight or more hours of sleep to function properly. Our health, safety, and performance depend on a good night's sleep. Yet, most procrastinators do not get the amount of sleep they should. There could be a good reason for this. Procrastinators tend to fear missing out on some kind of action. They think that if they sleep too long, they will miss out on something that they should have been involved in.

This is particularly true of college students. Procrastinators find that they delay studying until the last minute, and then they pull all-nighters and cram for the exams they need to take.

The problem with this is that they deprive themselves of sleep, which in turn affects their memory. When it comes time to take the test, they can't remember what they studied. This is why using good study habits and getting a good night's sleep is essential to passing exams and courses. Remember, it takes the brain twice as long to recover from fatigue as it does the body to recover from physical activity or exercise.

Many people wake up each morning by an alarm, which they set religiously, even though they don't have to get up so early. But what they fail to do is go to bed the night before in time to get a good night's sleep before that alarm goes off.

Sleep deprivation has caused many illnesses, problems, and even accidents. This is because when you have a lack of sleep, you can't concentrate fully. Not only can you not concentrate fully, but you also can't think quickly enough, nor can you remember facts or whatever material you had absorbed beforehand. It's true we can operate almost exclusively on an automatic subconscious level, but the conscious and subconscious minds are meant to work together in harmony, and not one above the other, or instead of the other.

What procrastinators need to realize is that when they go to bed at night, they won't miss anything. They will wake up feeling refreshed and ready to go and do whatever tasks they need to do. They will have a clear head and a better memory throughout the day, and they will be more successful at passing tests than if they sat up all night cramming.

The best way for procrastinators to avoid sleep deprivation is to set up a schedule to study and a schedule to sleep. By following this schedule religiously, they will find it easier to study and they won't miss the chance for a good night's sleep.

The best way to get the right amount of sleep, besides having a schedule of study, is to focus on going to bed at the same time each night and having a set time to get up in the morning. But don't set the clock to get you up too early in the morning until you have had ample time to get at least seven hours of sleep. If you must get up early, go to bed early, and do it each night. This way you will get the amount of sleep you need.

This will make you more alert, refreshed, and then ready to go for another day with more zeal. If you concentrate on doing this each day you will get into the habit of doing this and will then do it automatically. Then, with a little effort to keep the process going, you won't revert back to being a procrastinator again.

Whatever you do before you go to bed at night, don't drink caffeine or other stimulants. This is absolutely the worst thing to do. It acts as a stimulant and keeps you awake. If you must drink something hot, drink decaffeinated herbal tea or something less stimulating. If your procrastination is so advanced that nothing seems to work to help you sleep, go see a psychiatrist or psychologist, so you can begin to get the help you need.

You can deal with procrastination as long as you first know that you have it and that it is indeed a problem. Then you just need to learn about what causes the problem and then take steps to deal with it and make small progressive changes to produce a better You, and as a result, a better life.

Chapter Eight: Stop procrastinating now

In all the previous chapters you learned about some of the main causes of procrastination and why it happens. You were told that procrastination is a condition that can be cured once you know the condition, why it occurs, and how it happens. Knowing these facts will help you in your efforts to cure your procrastination.

So, what is there left to do? Well, you need to learn about the things you must do to stop procrastination in its tracks. A lot of the information you read in previous chapters will help you to deal with procrastination in addition to what follows.

In order to stop procrastinating, you must take certain steps and follow certain guidelines. Although you take the steps to stop procrastinating, remember that you have been procrastinating for a long time, so you aren't going to stop overnight. It will take some time to quit. Or rather, to get started. But if you work at a certain program every day, it will help lessen the effects of procrastination, until you are rid of it for good.

Taking small steps may be the best way to cure procrastination. But as suggested you must start slowly. Don't expect perfection, nor expect a change overnight. If you perform certain steps right, you'll eventually make it through to a procrastination-free life.

Here are the most recommended steps to take:

Start Small: Any time you do anything at first, your best bet is to start small. Take things gradually. If you must, make a list to follow each day. This will help you get through the day, at least till you don't have to be dependent on lists anymore.

Saying that, as you achieve small goals followed by medium-sized goals and eventually larger goals, you will want to make use of lists not because you need them, but because you want to make use of them in order to better track your progress and achieve even greater things in life beyond your current efforts to eliminate the procrastination habit.

Changing Home Life: The hardest part for procrastinators is living by themselves at home. There may be no one else around to say anything to them about their procrastination. This can cause them to lack self-discipline. In most cases, they will not want to even try to change, and the hardest part of being alone is changing! You have no one to encourage you or force you to keep going or make the necessary adjustments. This is why home life is the hardest area for a procrastinator to tackle. Most home activities are menial chores that keep you organized in order to build a better life experience. Home is really the foundation of a successful life.

The Control Factor: The biggest underlying problem for most procrastinators is that they like to take control of a situation whenever possible. Taking control has its good points and bad points. The good point is you see to it things get done. The bad point is that it can have negative connotations. You may develop the urge to go beyond the control you should have so instead, monitor your control and only do what is necessary to get the work done that needs to be done.

Don't go beyond that at first.

Have people around to help you so you won't have to go it alone. Using control can help you, especially in an office situation, but if you go beyond this control, you run the risk of jeopardizing the success of the project or situation. An example of this could be if there is a special meeting you have to go to by 1 p.m., but you also have reports that are due by 2 p.m.

You don't want to put off doing the reports. So, you get out your trusty list, and you work on your reports till about 12:30 p.m.

You then notice your meeting is in a building next door and it usually takes 10 minutes to get there. So, you work on the reports till 12:30 p.m. and then mark doing these reports off your list. Now you walk out the door and go to your meeting.

When you get back from the meeting, you check off the meeting from your list and take your reports to your manager for delivery. You have just completed your list for the day if that is all you had listed. If you had more, you simply go back to your office and continue down the list. This is the best way to use the proper and adequate amount of control. Simply and in a prioritized way.

Face Your Fears: The best way for anyone to face fears or resist the temptation to be a procrastinator is to think about what would happen to you if you procrastinated on the task you want to do. How would you feel about not doing it? What would happen if you didn't do it? Usually asking questions about your own fear and doubt is a way to break the fear. Because when you realize the fear is not real, it helps you to overcome it more easily.

Or, if you feel a lot of pain, anger, or resentment around the fear and avoidance you may face now, then perhaps you should think twice about allowing your procrastination to develop. Having this kind of general attitude has worked numerous times for procrastinators in the past and can work for you now if you let it work for you that is.

These are just some of the ways in which you can defeat and dump procrastination and so stop it in its tracks. Just take the necessary steps to alleviate it and you will soon find that it is soon to be a thing of the past. Imagine a life without having to suffer from procrastination. This is possible if you follow through on all you have to do and then stick to it. Remember, you can't get rid of procrastination overnight. It will take time, perhaps days, months, or even years, but you will eventually get rid of it.

First, once you have analyzed your life to discover where you procrastinate, get rid of those internal emotions that cause you to have procrastination like fear, avoidance, and perfectionism, and you'll soon be on your way to a life free of those emotions and conditions that have held you back for so long.

For the most part, the analyzing and setting of manageable goals is all that is required, just so long as you break down each of your projects and goals into smaller sub-projects and goals and break those down into manageable tasks.

Procrastination Summary

From reading this book you will have discovered that there are many people who suffer from procrastination in a variety of areas and ways, simply because it is a behavior problem that is very difficult to get rid of. People who suffer from it often find they engage in it without even thinking about it, it just happens to them and may drift in and out of it. Unfortunately, procrastination affects people in a bad way to such an extent that some people don't even know they have it.

The biggest question that is often asked is what actually is procrastination? As mentioned through this document, according to psychologists, procrastination is an avoidance of something. The person who is a procrastinator feels that his or her life is, or is becoming unmanageable. They will do everything possible to avoid situations, just so long as they can get out of facing their responsibility no matter what the task is. At first, the person is relieved to know no action had to be taken. But then feelings of guilt, inadequacy, depression, and self-doubt arise for failing to accomplish the task at hand.

Procrastination is a complex psychological behavior.

Those who are not afflicted by procrastination are lucky they don't have to deal with it. But then again, there are those who do have the condition and others that have it but not as bad as some people do. Some too suffer from it but they don't accept the fact that they do.

To those who are badly afflicted by it, the condition can lead to much stress and anxiety.

Procrastinators are often predictable in behavior; you give them a task and right away they are eager to do it. When they start the task, they think they have everything under control until they begin to do the work. Then they find they can't do it and make all kinds of excuses for not wanting to get it completed.

It is only when procrastinators can get in touch with the reality of their condition and then take steps in order to alleviate it, that their procrastination can become less of a burden, and maybe become a condition of the past.

For the person having the condition of procrastination, dealing with it is absolutely crucial. But many people try to treat the condition only to find it stays around and continues to haunt them. This is why the most important point here is to find the root cause or causes, and remove them so the person who suffers from it won't have to suffer on an ongoing basis and over the long term.

As was stated earlier, the causes of procrastination are many. These can include confusion and fear, not planning enough, not analyzing things, not prioritizing, avoiding responsibilities, chronic depression, fatigue, lack of vision, and many more symptoms. The three-step process I always recommend solves many of those issues and is available through the links at the end of this book.

So, now you know procrastination does not have to control your whole life and the eventual outcomes you experience.

Of course, if you have suffered from the effects of procrastination for a long time, it will be hard to get rid of. But it's not impossible. The main thing is to learn how to deal with it as we have suggested in this book so that once you fully understand how to deal with it, you can take the next step to get rid of the problem once and for all.

Before you can get rid of procrastination altogether, you have to acknowledge you have the problem. After you recognize that you have the condition, and in what areas of your life you are suffering because of it, you can then take the appropriate steps to rid yourself of its negative effects on your life.

There is one obstacle that stands in the way for many people. This is the fact that it could take a long time for it to be cured completely. Sometimes it can take days, weeks, or even years before the condition goes away completely. Once you understand the reasons behind procrastination, you can get to the root of it, and then remove that root cause, problem, or issue, which will, in turn, help you to remove procrastination more easily.

As you now know, the causes of procrastination are many and can vary from one person to another. It is hard to pinpoint the exact cause because there can be different origins for each person who suffers from it. The important thing to note here is that through analyzing each area of your life as suggested earlier you can then begin to solve the problem.

Procrastination may have deep-rooted causes which keep people from finding a cure for it right away. Even though the sufferer may have taken steps to cure themselves, unless the person gets to the core or root of the problem, they will likely have procrastination problems until such issues are dealt with. As long as the person has inner fear, a need for control, or a need for perfection, the person will continue to suffer from procrastination.

But procrastination can be dealt with. Those who suffer from it can be free of it. But as already suggested several times, in order to keep procrastination from becoming a major problem that persists, changes must be made on the inside first. Once these changes are made, any kind of problem that may have surfaced previously due to procrastination will be eliminated.

So, analyze your life and find the root cause of your personal procrastination so that you can create a vision for your life, set goals, make detailed step-by-step plans, organize and prioritize your life so you can achieve more than you ever thought possible. Once simple, doable step at a time.

Thanks for Listening.

Andy Raingold.

ELIMINATE THE NEGATIVES SERIES

FREEDOM FROM **ADDICTION**

HOW TO ELIMINATE ADDICTIONS, BAD HABITS, & BEHAVIOUR TO REGAIN COMPLETE CONTROL OF YOUR LIFE.

Written By:
Andy Raingold

Graphic Design By: Stephen Hawkins.
Special Thanks To Nathanial Dasco & Ikhide Oshoma

ADDICTION INTRODUCTION

Even from the earliest times, addiction has been a big, constant problem for some people - from drug addiction to smoking and gambling, to food addiction, sexual addiction, or even internet addiction. These kinds of addictions are a growing problem and there have been many studies on how to overcome all of these problems.

But somehow, the problem still remains and persists. And in fact, it even evolves into something much bigger and more difficult to conquer, which means that there are addictions that are actually harder to overcome now, especially with the recent advent of technology. People have become even more resourceful, they have also become more inventive and more prone to dealing with addictions that are sometimes not subject to scrutiny.

So, if you are addicted to something, what do you need to do to deal with it? How do you overcome addiction before it overcomes you? Or the better question, do you think you even need help?

This short book answers these questions and much more as it delves into a deeper meaning of what addiction is from a purely practical perspective and how it originally started. This book shows some examples of the different kinds of addictions, both the usual and the unusual so you can analyze yourself and your own life to make sure you are not acting against your own best interests.

It follows the usual patterns of an addiction victim - from the most common to the most unusual addiction problem. And it tackles the causes of addiction - why some people are hooked on these kinds of things and why it is hard for them to stop.

And still, the bottom line is, it has got to stop.

Because not only will addictions destroy your life, they can lead to broken families and relationships, accidents, suffering, or even death.

And that is one effect of addiction that you wouldn't want to experience for yourself or your loved ones.

This book serves to help you overcome all of these addictions so that you or your family might experience the victory and success you rightfully deserve.

I approach this in two ways. First, the more theoretical scientific approach that is included in this second book in the series. Second through my own observations and experiences as well as perspective. This is covered in the next book in the series which of course follows Freedom from Addiction. It is titled eliminate The Negatives. So, for now, let's move on and begin to dig deeper into the currently known or perhaps unknown addictive behavior you or a loved one may currently be living with using the theoretical approach.

Chapter One: WHAT IS ADDICTION AND HOW DOES IT BEGIN?

What Is Addiction?

Addiction has been an age-old problem for many people. From the time of our ancestors to the time of new technologies cropping up today, addiction has always been there but is not really fully addressed because it is getting very rampant and very hard to control.

But the question still remains: What really is an addiction? How do you define it? How does it begin and how do you know if you are already addicted to something?

Addiction is a recurring compulsion of some particular substance or activity that keeps on happening at any time of the day. It is a dependence on a behavior or a substance that a person feels powerless to stop. It is automatic programmed behavior.

The term has been partially replaced by the word dependence in the case of such addictions as substance abuse. Addiction has been extended, however, to include mood-altering behaviors or activities, that in the end, all addictions are meant to achieve.

Some researchers speak of two types of addictions: substance addictions (for example, alcoholism, drug abuse, and smoking); and process addictions (for example, gambling addiction, overspending, shopping, eating, and sexual activity addictions). In other words, addiction is a term often used to describe someone who is dependent on something. Unlike in the past, when addiction was associated mainly with drugs, addiction now also includes different forms such as gambling, smoking, drinking, food, and even sex.

Here are a couple of questions that you should ask yourself to determine if you are addicted to a substance or a behavior:

Do you often feel that you may have compulsions or a substance addiction problem?

Do you think a lot about your compulsions or substance of choice?

Do the compulsions or chemical substances seem necessary to have a good time, feel good, or to fit in?

Have you ever felt guilty or ashamed about your compulsions or using this substance?

Have you ever used your compulsions or chemical substance to mask your emotional pain?

Do you continue your compulsions or do you use a chemical substance despite negative consequences?

Have you stolen in order to accommodate your compulsion or to buy your substance of choice?

Are your compulsions or your substance of choice disrupting your general family life or relationships?

Has your job, career, or school performance suffered from your compulsions or substance abuse?

Have you ever lied about your compulsions?

Have you ever tried to stop your compulsions?

Does it seem impossible to live without them?

Are you having/have you ever had withdrawal symptoms after attempting to stop using any substance?

Do your compulsions and/or use of substances affect your general behavior?

Do you depend on any substance to help you through the day?

If you answered yes to any of these questions, then you might be struggling right now with an addiction problem.

The medical community now makes a theoretical differentiation between physical dependency and psychological dependency. But in recent years, medical experts have now bridged the gap between these two differences to come up with the very same meaning for addiction.

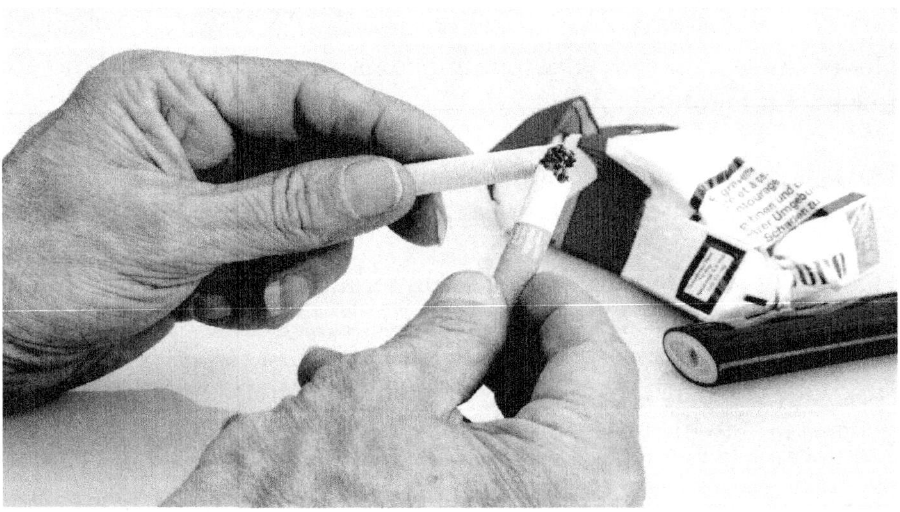

People who are addicted to something have both physical symptoms and they also have compulsive behaviors. They act on something without even thinking of the consequences.

But with these definitions, let us now narrow it down and discuss the two common forms of addiction - physical dependency and psychological dependency.

Physical dependency means that when a person is addicted to something and then when the addictive substance is suddenly withdrawn or discontinued, the person suffers physical pain and discomfort.

Although the role of addiction is usually seen as a way to induce pleasure, this is not necessarily so.

In fact, one purpose of addiction is to reduce anxiety or panic in a person, and on the physical level, this means avoiding the pain of withdrawal symptoms. One of these examples is nicotine, which is a drug found in cigarettes and some other drugs. Users have reported that they experience extreme pleasure when drawing on a cigarette, which is relative to his or her psychological state.

Furthermore, the physical dependency of a person engaged in nicotine use makes it a lot harder for him to quit smoking since the substance itself is quite addictive.

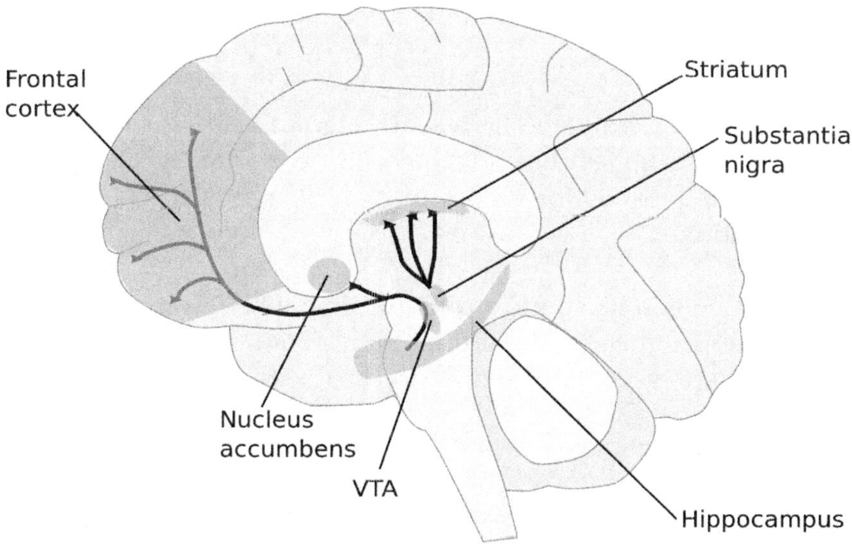

As for psychological dependency, it leads to various psychological syndromes such as irritability, anxiousness, depression, anorexia, bulimia, and others.

In this case, addiction can actually be attributed to what is known as the dopaminergic system, or the brain's ability or lack of ability to produce dopamine, a pleasure-inducing substance.

This kind of psychological factor is considered as a way to escape the realities of life, especially within the individual who may have psychological, emotional, or social dysfunctions. Psychological dependence can involve behaviors such as the general overuse of computers, the internet, pornography, gaming, and many other types of addictions.

There is actually very little difference between physical and psychological dependency as far as the results are concerned. The difference lies in the causes and characteristics of each of these two types, and with the types of treatment that are being used for each of them.

How Does Addiction Begin?

Contrary to what many might think, addiction basically starts in the mind and the emotions

that you feel. See Eliminate The Negatives in this series. In life, there are trials and struggles that you have to deal with every day but there are some persons for whom these trials seem to be too much to handle at times.

This kind of person has quite a difficult time when dealing with the negative things that are besetting him. Emotions such as pain, discomfort, depression, and anxiety overcome him or her.

This person basically starts out just like any ordinary person - as a normal individual who is not being influenced by anything. When trials and problems come their way, such as fitting in with a group as a child or as a teenager, a confrontation within his family, the loss of a career, the loss of a loved one, or even low grades in school, this person is submerged by negative emotions and may feel unloved and unworthy of love.

When a person experiences these kinds of discomforts, they feel that it is unendurable and unmanageable. They see no solution to all of these experiences and resort to something that could take away all of these pains forever.

And so, the influence begins - from their friends, from society, even from the media.

From experience and from the usual conversations with people who are influenced by all kinds of things, addiction usually begins with just a look, smell, feel or touch and then a taste - a taste of a "better" life experience, if only a perceived one.

In other words, it starts out with just being a little curious. Once a pleasant and blissful feeling overcomes them, then they would like to taste it again, over and over again. Until it becomes an "addiction."

This addiction isn't necessarily focused on drugs, but there are other types of addictions that people fall into in an attempt to take away all of their problems - such as cigarette and alcohol addiction, internet, and gambling addictions, as well as sex, which has also come to be considered as an addiction under certain circumstances.

When this person engages in the addictive substance or behavior, he or she feels relieved because the pleasure is there - these addictions have finally relieved the person of the discomfort he or she feels. Or have they?

Their addictions now become so important to them because they make them feel better. After they have tried it several times, it becomes an addiction and finally, they lose their ability to control the use of these substances or their behavior.

Addictions, no matter what they are, result from over excessive or continuous use of a substance or behavior to hide or remove the negative emotions that a person feels inside, such as depression, pain, anxiety, panic, or feelings of unworthiness.

And so, for a person who is suffering all of these struggles and problems, being addicted to something seems to be the real answer - a dangerous answer that could overcome not only a person's physical well-being, but it could affect his relationships with others, his heart, and his personality.

Various Explanations on Addiction

Aside from the ones discussed above which consider the aspects of psychological and physical dependency, there are also several models which scientists have proposed that might explain how addiction begins and why people become hooked. There are models which explain that addictions also have physiological and psycho-social factors.

Here are a couple of explanations of why addiction happens. Again, see Eliminate The Negatives for my personal experiences with addiction and my eventual, permanent cure.

The disease model

In this model, addiction is considered an illness, resulting from a disruption of the behavioral and neurochemical processes. This disease can be treated by specialists and experts. It is argued that in this case, those suffering from addiction have either a physical or mental illness to some extent.

For some, the problem stems from the inability of addictive persons to produce dopamine in their brain and then seek to replace this lack by using various substances. Genita Petralli H.H.P., N.C., M.H., says *"The home of alcoholism resides in the hypothalamus, pituitary, adrenal axis and only through balancing the functional neuroendocrine system can one naturally feel good inside their own skin again."*

For others, the root cause is a mineral deficiency. Linus Pauling said, "*You can trace every sickness, every disease and every ailment to a mineral deficiency*" Dr. Joel Wallach has also spoken and written extensively on this subject, affirming that all addictions are a form of Pica, a craving for minerals that leads some people to ingest dirt and other substances.

For naturopathic doctor Hulda Clark, the cause of addictions is food contaminated with ergot (a toxic mold) and the ingestion, usually through breathing, of the toxic substance beryllium, which is found in kerosene and coal products. These toxins affect the brain, causing cravings for different substances.

The genetic model

There is also a model which is called the genetic model, which states that there is actually a predisposition to certain types of behaviors and personalities.

It is said that addiction is based on heredity and that it basically *"runs in the family."* Experts and scientists are still studying this factor but they believe that the family or certain relationships can contribute to addiction and that they have a lasting influence on the addict.

The experiential model

Stanton Peele devised a model called the experiential model which asserts that addiction is actually related to experiences outside the home, whether it has something to do with positive or negative factors. Aside from that, it also says that addiction can still be outgrown through a purely natural process and is actually temporary.

The opponent-process model

This model, devised by Richard Soloman, states that if there is a psychological "event A", for example, then there will follow a psychological "event B". An example of this would be if a person is addicted to drugs, the result of this might be withdrawal from his family and from his relationships. In the same way, in a simpler illustration, if a person is concerned with being in small, enclosed spaces, that person might refuse to get inside an elevator.

This model can also be associated with the color process scheme, in which if a person looks at the color red long enough and then looks at the color gray, he will see green.

Other instances of the opponent-process model are those involving the sensory systems such as taste, sight, touch, and smell. The opponent-process system might translate the sensory stems into addiction or something habit-forming.

A variation of this model, designed by George Koob and Michael

LeMoal, is called stability through change, where it modifies the opponent-process model by Richard Soloman. In this model, the continued use of drugs or any substance may lead to other symptoms such as uncontrolled usage, withdrawal, or negative emotions.

The cultural model

In this model, the culture or where a person grows up or is transferred to might have a greater impact on addiction. An example would be the case of liquor, which is prohibited in some countries such as Saudi Arabia. This would then reduce the liquor addiction of some people.

On the other hand, in the United States of America, gambling addiction has soared to new heights in recent decades, with the influence of some cities which allow gambling. There have also been studies in which liquor addiction gained ground in some families because liquor is prevalent in their households.

On the other hand, people who are born into families where liquor is present in moderation may have more resistance to alcoholism.

The moral model

As the name suggests, this model holds that addiction comes from a defect in the human character. Those who have this type of prototype believe that there is no biological basis for addiction. They can empathize with people who have suffered addiction in their lives but still hold them morally responsible.

As the name suggests, this model holds that addiction comes from a defect in the human character. Those who have this type of prototype believe that there is no biological basis for addiction. They can empathize with people who have suffered addiction in their lives but still hold them morally responsible.

The habit model

Suggested by Thomas Szasz argues against the very theory of "addiction." He states that the only way to tell the difference between a habit and addiction is *"just to make someone perish."*

The blended model

Proposes a different therapeutic treatment to each and every addiction for each individual and considers that these individuals must be regarded and treated separately.

The above examples are just some proposals and suggestions as to why a person gets addicted to a particular substance or behavior. Until now, scientists, psychologists, and experts are still debating on how addiction begins - whether it is influenced by the family, by the culture, or by the environment. They have devoted their time, energy, and effort to solving this age-old problem.

Conquering addiction starts from the heart and no matter what new technology crops up nowadays, how a person deals with his problems or trials in life makes all the difference. The more negative his perception, the more he will become addicted to something. The more positive, the better he is able to cope with these problems.

Chapter Two: PATTERNS OF ADDICTION

Addiction Patterns

There are many variations of addiction and there are some which are manifested in very, very different ways. Below are some ways in which addictions can be manifested in a person and his life. These manifestations are combined, varied, and interlocked at times and they overlap each other, which is one reason why addiction can be a difficult habit to break.

Resistance and Avoidance

Addictions contain a feel-good factor in that they deliver the person from their current painful experiences. But with addiction, everything that is accessible to a person's view is an addiction, especially when it serves as an instrument for resistance and avoidance of the pain that this person feels inside. Even the worst situations, such as cutting up oneself or flagellation can become addictive.

The person usually starts out by feeling the pleasure or the fascination of doing something over and over again and then they begin to find out quite "accidentally" that this pleasure or dark fascination actually has some benefits - and keeps them from the pain and the struggles that they experience in everyday living. And it also anesthetizes their consciousness.

And then they begin to indulge in a substance less for the pleasure but more for the results, to be able to keep the ache and the pains of the body and general living away.

And when addiction becomes a compulsion, then they begin to resort to greater heights and levels of use in order to keep the bad pains or feelings away.

Obviously, taking drugs is the most common form of addiction but whether it be ordinary and common stuff such as biting your nails, compulsive shopping, or even using your cell phone for most of the day when these are something you feel that you should or indeed need to do, then it becomes a pattern.

The solution would be to ask yourself what would happen if you suddenly stopped this behavior. The real question would be: Are you willing to stop? Can you stop doing this even for just a minute? If you feel that you can't, then there is really a pattern. But if you tried to stop these addictions, what is the first thing that you would feel? Well, the most obvious would be that if you stop doing one or all of these things, then there is that immediate feeling of fear.

This is actually the fear that tells you that if you stop doing this, something bad will eventually happen and then the pain will recur once more. The things that make you feel bad are the things that probably happened to you a long time ago with relationships or the things that you have been avoiding for so long that you can't deal with them.

The Needy Baby

There is a part within each one of us that still thinks that we are a "baby" and that we still need nourishment from our parents, from our friends, and from our relationships. Even if you have the most wonderful parents in the world who have been taking care of you ever since you were a child, there can still be an amount of pain inside you that you want to voice out but nobody seems to be listening, or want to listen to you.

There are instances where you receive messages that tell you to stop doing that, to suppress your feelings, or just literally, to grow up. These messages seem a little bit harsh but even if it was done in the gentlest manner, we can feel angry and attacked inside, and when we express all of these as inner children, there is never a positive response from others. This heightens the angry needy child within and this results in a response of anger and judgment.

So, in effect, what then happens to all of these parts which haven't been completely healed yet? What happens to these parts which are harboring a state of denial and which are having a hard time expressing all of these needy baby feelings? The most obvious outcome would be for this person to hide his true feelings and resort to "hiding."

They try to get their needs filled with an outward stimulus that seems pleasurable and delectable. This is where they try to pour out their feelings and express them in negative ways. What they do is really simple: they try to assign labels to people, places, and things that tell them that these are the things that they really need and that if they can have these things, then they will be satisfied and happy.

But of course, all of these things are not really eternal. They are just temporary. What the needy baby can do is to cry fully so that he can heal old wounds and, in this way, he can bring out all the negative feelings that are stored inside. When this happens, the needy baby can be nurtured and fed, and there are several ways in which to fulfill the needs of the needy baby. The pain and the hurt would then gradually diminish.

Prisoner of War

In this kind of addictive pattern, the subconscious feels detached from the other parts of the personality and feels that it is being judged.

It feels that it is separated from the parts that matter, such as the heart, the mind, the soul, and the divine. When this kind of feeling dominates, it's as if the whole weight of anxiety, panic, depression, repression, suppression, and weightlessness creeps in. It looks as if there is actually no way out.

When all of these things happen, the subconscious now becomes angry and there is hatred in its heart. He backs up into one corner of the room and now becomes a prisoner of war, a child who is hungry for the situations that would make him feel better. The subconscious then starts to take itself wherever it can find enjoyable feelings - whatever the cost and whatever the pleasure is.

The conscious mind then enters into direct conflict with the subconscious but when the mind does this, the subconscious often takes control over the situation. Drug addicts usually experience this kind of situation - sort of like a feeling of being "unconscious" such as gorging on a piece of cake without even realizing it, going from one department store to another, and buying everything that you think you need without even realizing it, or spending too much money on betting on something without being aware of it.

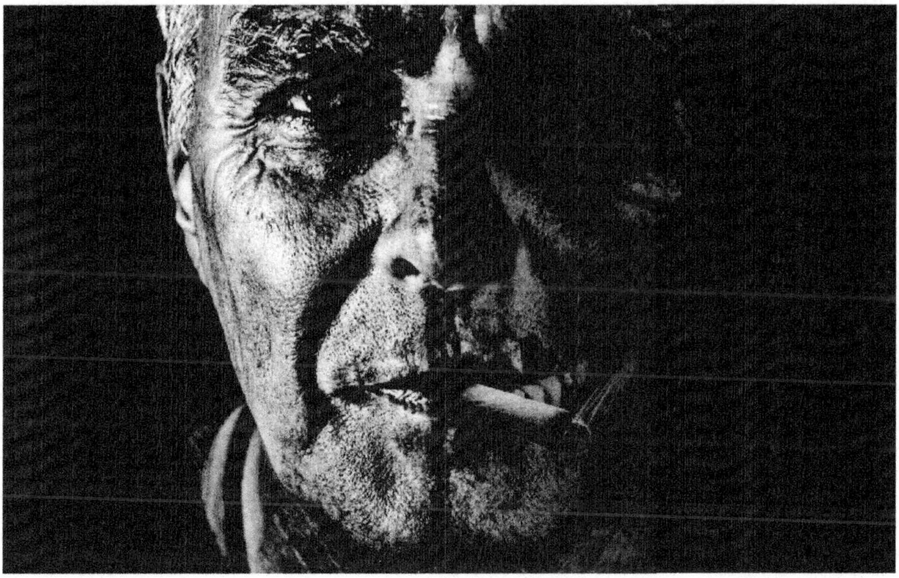

There are two pleasurable things that the "prisoner of war" benefits from here. The first is the obvious enjoyment of food, drugs, gambling, shopping, spending, or whatever. But the second feeling that this person experiences, is a feeling of control, that he is able to "steal" something and be in control.

This person actually experiences great power in the process of stealing something, despite how morbid, despite how appalling it could be, and even up to the point of putting the life of this person in great danger. For this person, possessing that great power is pleasurable.

Self-Hatred / Death Wish

There are various faces of self-hatred but addiction is considered the most sinister. Obviously, the things that we are addicted to are not really good for our bodies and spirits. Whether things are taken in small amounts or in large amounts or being constantly taken, it could lead to addiction. Self-hatred is quite similar to a little devil on our shoulder egging us on and encouraging us to take more of that substance. This little devil whispers sweet nothings in our ears and even gives out negative comments if you don't follow his orders to be fulfilled. His techniques are based on the thought that you are too weak and too vulnerable to resist, and he keeps taunting us to go on with this type of addiction. When this happens, it really gets very nasty.

This little voice in our heads then exceeds the boundaries and tries another tactic: that of telling us that we are awful, bad, horrible, dumb, and all kinds of negative things.

If we have a drug problem or a liquor problem, this little devil inside us gathers all the bad information about what you have done under the influence and this will serve as his weapon to nag you later on.

The self-hatred becomes destructive, to the point of having a death wish being repeated in your ear. Even though the death wish in itself is outside your consciousness, it delivers in more ways than one and tries to fulfill your death wish after all.

The worst kinds of scenarios in terms of addiction are those that give us pleasure at the onset and then drag us down to the pit until we begin to feel depressed and death now becomes your number one priority, or at the very least, an option. But of course, it isn't.

Chipping

This pattern of addiction basically means that the person is not really dependent on a substance but the person still maintains a "controlled" usage of the drug. This is implemented by avoiding the major addictive influences that could contribute to this drug dependence, such that the drug is mostly used for relaxation and rejuvenation and not escape. There is a common term for this - recreational substance use.

Family Patterns - The Dry Drunk Pattern

A dry drunk is a recovered alcoholic who is no longer physically addicted to alcohol, but who still manifests certain behavioral patterns common to alcoholics. Take note that the dry drunk patterns that are mentioned here are not only exclusive to those with liquor problems but to those with drug problems as well. These addictive patterns may also be inherited from previous generations.

Here are some traits which are considered "dry drunk" behavioral patterns.

- A firm and judgmental viewpoint on life
- Irresponsibility
- Being impatient
- Pretentious lifestyle
- Illogical rationalization
- Childish behavior
- Exaggerated self-worth
- Defensiveness
- Insistence on being correct all the time, even when his reasoning is wrong.

These traits describe the addict, whether or not he is drinking, gambling, or high on drugs. The person who is a "dry drunk" basically has control over his behavior but has not changed his attitude.

It is actually the emotional factors that are quite essential and important here. There is a possibility that the patterns of the Needy Baby and Self-Hatred may be combined here. This pattern requires the family to focus on the "addict" himself and when the situation isn't corrected by understanding and treating the "sickness" pattern of the addict, then the real issue isn't really addressed.

Family Coping Patterns

There are children who try to cope in a seemingly addictive world that is slightly similar to their parents. They try to be safe and sane in an insane world.

Here are some common coping patterns that children utilize:

Being a Hero and a Responsible Child. Owning up to their own responsibilities makes children displace all their mixed feelings and energies, whether positive or negative, into an outward stimulus such as sports, recreation, school work, partying, and being able to achieve everything.

In doing all of these things, the hero or responsible child takes the attention away from the family problems and instead, it even makes the family look good since he is the one taking charge. The only flaw here is that this is only temporal and is not lasting - the hero/responsible child can never feel good for a long time even though he exceeds in everything. He must admit that even he can't fix the problems of the family.

Scapegoat. There are reasons and purposes why children become delinquents, rebellious, or attention-grabbing at some point in their lives. These attitudes that they portray may divert attention from the real problem of the family: the dependence on this particular substance. The child, who is treated as a scapegoat in the family, may wind up in some cycle of despair and frustration. He acts out to show his frustration, and when he gets blamed for everything, the frustration doesn't diminish - the frustration heightens. Other feelings such as anger, guilt, and inadequacy also begin to surface as a result.

The Actor. There are some children who like to play with masks - hiding their true feelings and coping with their parents' addictions by feeling happy and joyful.

This attitude may seem to take away the problems of the family with addiction but in reality, it masks the true behaviors of the family.

The Lost Child. This is somewhat the opposite of being an actor in the family. There are some children who cope with the addiction in the family by being withdrawn and lost and trying to be always by themselves most of the time. They actually deny what they feel inside and deny that they are faced with any problems and instead they feel that they are undetectable.

How to Break Your Addiction

The real issue here is that you should try to admit that you have a problem with addiction so that real healing can take effect. It's important to shout out the pain in order that these dangerous and destructive behaviors can eventually stop. But take caution: if you try to stop the addiction by force or suddenly, be forewarned that you might be shifting to another kind of addiction. It's possible that you might go from being a smoking addict to a workaholic or to a gambling addict.

In order that the pattern may be changed and in order to stop this addiction completely, you must get to the root of the problem. Being addicted to a substance is just the surface of the iceberg - the real problem lies underneath. There is a real reason why a person is addicted to a substance.

As mentioned above, there are several patterns associated with addiction. These people usually have addictive personalities, and it's very difficult to break free from these patterns. It feels as if there is a strong current that is leading you in the wrong direction.

It is easier to go with the flow than fight against the current. Don't get me wrong - self-control is not the main issue here. There are people who quit their addictions more easily, probably because they have fewer problems to deal with, while for many others it is very difficult. It's important not to pass negative judgment on anyone. Including yourself.

As seen above, there are different interpretations about the causes of addiction, and therefore different theories about what must be done to heal them. Some put emphasis on physical factors; others are more prone to consider the psychological aspects. In devising a program to cure your own addiction or to help a loved one, it would be best to cover all of your bases by paying attention to both the physical and the emotional aspects. They are not contradictory, but complementary.

The Physical Aspect

In today's Western society, the body and the mind are often seen as two separate entities that are entirely independent of each other.

But we now know that our bodies are constantly secreting various substances that have an effect on our mood. We also know that addiction is often the ingestion of a mood-altering substance.

So, it's not far-fetched at all to imagine that an addicted person is trying desperately to obtain something that is missing inside of him on a strictly physical level, although there could be a parallel on the emotional level that gives even more strength to the person's compulsion.

Nutrition

And so, a good place to start would be to examine your diet and find some good nutritional supplements that provide the full range of vitamins and minerals, including trace minerals.

Of course, you also want to eat healthy food. People who are addicted to alcohol or drugs have notoriously poor eating habits. But good food is not enough. Someone who has not eaten well for a long time needs the extra boost of supplements.

Toxic substances

We live in a polluted environment. The problem is that some people can tolerate a higher level of pollution than others. The addicted person's body may be affected by certain substances that would not bother others.

It may require a lot of patient detective work to examine your environment to find the culprit (or culprits).

Are you exposed to particular substances through your job or leisure activities? Look in particular for the presence of the element beryllium, which Hulda Clark holds as responsible for addictions.

Parasites

Who would want to be a host to those yucky little critters, whether or not you're addicted to anything? Treat the whole family. You can try natural remedies, such as black walnut hulls, or try Hulda Clark's zapper. Just do what is necessary to get rid of them. Remember, the symptoms of their presence can be vague and might not be detected by a regular medical examination.

The psychological aspect

Get Help

Some of the emotional factors involved in addictions were mentioned above, but it is beyond the scope of this book to treat this highly complex subject in-depth, and anyone with a serious addiction problem needs one-on-one care that only a professional can give. So, the first and most important piece of advice here is: don't try to go it alone.

Whether it is you or a close loved one that is suffering from an addiction, you need support. Reading this book is a good first step, and hopefully, it will give some useful information as well as encouragement, but nothing can replace personal contact.

Find A Support Group. In addition to a doctor and/or therapist, a support group can be a great help. There are people like you who have the same addiction problems and it's much easier to tell all your problems to them since they can relate to you.

One of the best and most well-known of these groups is Alcoholics Anonymous, but there are others. Look for one where you feel comfortable. These groups can give you a sense of belonging and help you to feel that you are not alone, and they can also impart advice and new ideas to help you. And don't forget the Eliminate The Negatives book in this series.

Alternative Methods

A classical psychotherapist may be just the person you need, but be aware that there are many other useful methods out there. Some require a specialist or therapist, such as Hypnotherapy, Reiki, Kinesiology, Subliminal, Acupuncture, and Homeopathy. Others you can try alone, although they might be more effective with a qualified therapist. Some of these are NLP (neuro-linguistic programming), EFT (emotional freedom technique), and even Reflexology. You can also add Affirmations to your regime.

You will note that alternative methods cannot always be classified as belonging to either the physical or the emotional category, because they act on the body and the mind simultaneously. The point is that external as well as self-help methods work together.

Helping Yourself

This may seem to be in contradiction to the above paragraphs, but it's not. Getting help is not the same thing as being totally passive. If you have appendicitis, you go to the hospital, they put you to sleep and take out your appendix. It's a very passive affair, and quite appropriate for that case. But with addictions, you've got a lot of work ahead of you, and the people that you find to help you are there to help and encourage you to take the proper action and take responsibility for your life. They can't do it for you; they can only help you.

Below you will find a few suggestions of how you can take some action to help yourself:

Make a choice. Whenever you consciously decide to change an aspect of your life or eliminate a negative such as an addiction, your whole being gets involved and either fights you on the matter or supports you. It is important that your determination to be victorious is backed by these decisions. If needs be, make the same choice several times over and your subconscious will eventually get the message that you mean business. You are in effect telling yourself that you mean business.

Take one step at a time. Try to reduce the addiction just for a short while until you feel the pain of the withdrawal beginning to surface. While you feel that pain, pose the intention to let go of it.

You can repeat this over a longer period of time.

Explore your feelings and let out all the emotions that you feel inside - cry out the pain, feel the pain and all the hurt, and even try to express your anger (of course, not too violently, just for yourself - punch a pillow so to speak).

Then take a few deep, quiet breaths. Try to feel the place in your body where your addiction lies and try to feel whether it has lessened. When you start to feel it being lessened, see if you can wait a little longer before you take a cigarette or drink a glass of wine. Eventually, you'll find that the addiction is gradually shifting by itself.

Go on to another form of feeding spree. Let the "baby" cry out to express his feelings - along with all the hurt, pain, anger, and loneliness. Let him speak to you and find some other things to nurture your "baby", things that you enjoy but that are not destructive.

Shift to Another Addiction. This might seem like a ridiculous resolution to an addiction problem but this could really work.

While you are dealing with a present addiction, there may come a point where your need for this will eventually loosen but you aren't ready to let it go. Try to substitute a different addiction that is less destructive.

An example would be an alcoholic who continues to smoke or a smoker who turns to food and gains weight.

The root problem of the addictive personality traits is not solved, (I go into this in the Eliminate The Negatives book) and the new addiction is less than ideal, but you are moving in the right direction by substituting a lesser evil for a more destructive one.

Be Active. Do a little bit of something which interrupts your basic addiction process. Go for a brisk walk, try a new hobby or go out with a couple of friends for fun and enjoyment. Try something you have never done before. Get your awareness away from the addiction and instead focus on your body and get away from the pain and the desire that you feel whenever you indulge in that addiction.

However, a warning: this solution is just temporary. You must get to the root of the problem and not just cure the symptoms.

Meditate. As much as possible, try to make contact with the inner light within you and meditate. Embrace the light as it wraps you and fulfills you. If you feel that you are now loved, worthy, hopeful, you are on your way to recovery and gradually beating the addiction. Even if this only strengthens your resolve.

Imagining that you have all these feelings within you is really a way to get all of your feelings of unworthiness to slowly vanish. And this is essential in dealing with your addictions.

Do A General "House Cleaning." Remove all the stuff from your house that could trigger your addiction, such as cigarettes, liquor, gambling cards, and others. As much as possible, you can ask a friend or a family member to help you do this.

Make sure that your body is getting what it needs. Remember the three vital factors in achieving a healthy body: eat a balanced diet, exercise, and get enough sleep and rest. Take vitamin and mineral supplements, as mentioned previously, especially if you are addicted to drugs and with alcohol addiction.

Drink plenty of water also. Water helps in cleaning out the toxins in your body systems.

Be Prepared. Be prepared, especially for withdrawal symptoms. If you are facing addictions such as drugs or alcohol, know what the symptoms of withdrawal are and prepare what you need to do in advance. Also, prepare your family and friends by informing them of what you are going through right now - you might become irritable in the days to come because of this withdrawal. If you think that these withdrawal symptoms can be treated, go see a doctor or a nutritionist.

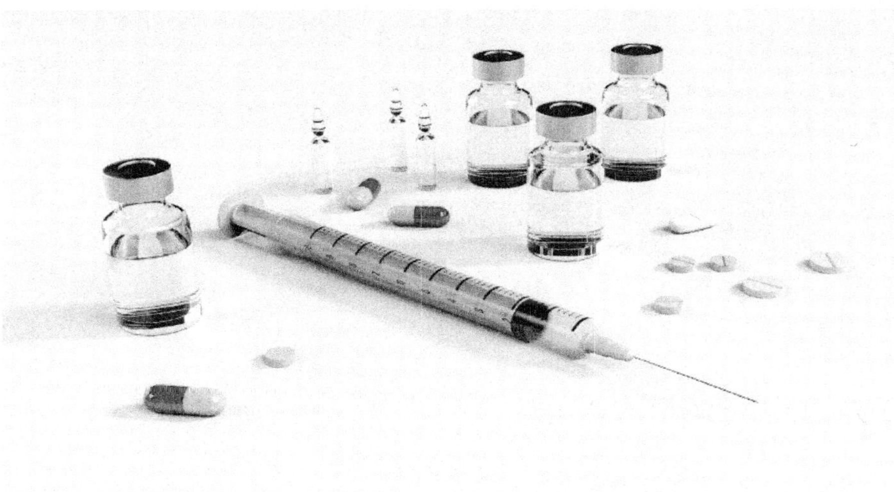

You can also prepare some activities to take your focus off of the addiction/symptoms. Read or write a book or start a new project, create a website - something that interests you.

Help Other People with the Same Problem. We spoke earlier about support groups. In your support group, you will find that it is a two-way street. Not only are they helping you, but you will find that you have something that they need and that will help them. This will increase your sense of self-esteem and help you to find meaning in the middle of your suffering.

Chapter Three: COMMON ADDICTIONS, CAUSES, AND CURES

Drug Addiction

Even though we all know what drug addiction means and this addiction needs no introduction, we may still benefit from asking the question: what is drug addiction? Many of us have taken drugs in our lives. There are drugs that are prescribed by doctors, such as painkillers, anti-depressants, and drugs that treat various diseases and disorders. Many of these legal drugs will create dependencies, physical and/or psychological.

When we speak of addictions, we are referring to a situation where the drug is not necessary for the person and where it does more harm than good.

There are two components of drug addiction that have been mentioned earlier: basic physical dependency and psychological dependency. Physical dependency is the state of physical being wherein a person takes the drug continuously and where the body is already used to the effects of the drug. The effects of this are that the person must continue using the drug, or else he will feel pain or discomfort.

Psychological dependency, on the other hand, is a lot more subtle and more dangerous than physical dependency since it not only involves the body but the mind as well. Just like the body, when the mind is involved, the drug frees the mind of the pain and replaces it with extreme pleasure, so the user doesn't feel able to cope without using it.

When the drug is not in use, more cravings are produced, which are usually heightened when the person feels more stressed.

The Disease Model of Drug Addiction

The cause of drug addiction, according to this theory, is that it is a form of dysfunctional learning. Certain drugs take control of neurological functions involving reward and motivation, which leads to aberrant learning.

According to an article on the Duke University website, *"exposure to cocaine triggers changes in a brain region called the striatum -- a reward center that also plays a fundamental role in movement and emotional responses. Cocaine leads to a sharp increase in communication among nerve cells in the striatum that use dopamine as their chemical messenger. This brain chemical surge is responsible for the feeling of pleasure, or high, that leads drug users to crave more. Since this has a huge effect on the physical body, drug abuse now becomes involuntary, with the immediate desire in seeking more of the pleasure feelings through these drugs."*

One of the effects of taking drugs is long-term depression (LTD) in brain circuits that are associated with the process of addiction, suggesting that addictive behavior may become reinforced by learning mechanisms.

The Reward System

Drugs are classified and work in different ways. The reward and pleasure exhibited from these drugs also vary.

Depressants such as benzodiapines and alcohol function by

heightening the affinity of the receptor of its ligand, GABA. Narcotics, such as methadone and morphine, work by imitating endorphins - chemicals that are produced in the body. These substances are also called "downers" in that they take away the pain and promote relaxation.

Stimulants such as nicotine, amphetamines, and cocaine actually boost the signal of dopamine in two ways: either by stimulating the release of it or by blocking the absorption of it. These stimulants, called "uppers" cause an increased level of energy and awareness in an individual. The effects give the person a different high but after its effects have worn off, the person feels depressed or down again. This causes the person to want to take the drug again and again.

There have been many prescriptions or over-the-counter drugs which can be addictive if they are not used properly. Medications that involve steroids, for example, are tremendously addictive, as well as sleeping tablets, such as valium. There are also drugs that are not available over the counter and are not considered to have medical value at all which can be considered addictive. As far as addiction is concerned, these drugs may be legal for government study but they may be illegal to sell, illegal to use, or even illegal to possess.

Former president of the United States Richard Nixon, in 1972, even issued a memorandum to stamp out drug addiction and to stop crimes that are connected to drugs. But today the problem is still rampant, with the additional problem that when these addicts don't have enough money to support their habit, they often turn to crime.

Drug Addiction Recovery

There are several methods to treat drug addiction and there are lots of factors to consider - such as the amount of drugs used, how long the individual has been addicted to the drug, medical complications, and the needs of the individual. Treatment is essential to the drug addict as well as to the people who are in constant contact with this person.

There are organizations in the United States and around the world such as Narcotics Anonymous, which helps individuals along the same lines as Alcoholics Anonymous in facing their problems, using the 12-step recovery program. They not only aid in helping out the drug addict but they get to the root of the problem, as discussed in a previous chapter. And in other ways, there are also substance rehabilitation centers or rehab centers that help drug addicts by isolating them from drugs and from those people who influence them to take drugs.

There are also outpatient clinics that offer both individual counseling and group counseling. Usually, there is a physician or a specialized doctor to help in prescribing medications that could help the drug addict in dealing with the problem (the most frequent symptom that these medications can help is anxiety).

Cognitive-Behavioral Theory

Some rehab centers in the US and also in the UK have been offering a variety of treatment programs for drug addicts. They use Cognitive-Behavioral Theory (CBT), which looks at the relationship between thoughts, feelings, and attitudes, being aware that a change in these areas affects the whole individual.

CBT looks at addiction as a behavior and not as a disease and therefore, it is curable and doctors involved in this program see the real possibility of healing.

Replacement Drugs

There are also other ways to control drug addiction, such as replacing the drug with another drug, and one of these drugs is methadone. Methadone itself is quite addictive, but it is used because it is considered less harmful to the person than heroin, and can be legally administered by doctors.

Alternative therapies

Chiropractic adjustments, surprisingly, have been found effective in combination with other treatments. These adjustments can help by restoring the normal functioning of the nervous system that had been disturbed by misaligned joints.

Some other alternative treatments include acupuncture, herbal medicine, hypnotherapy, creative visualization, biofeedback, and homeopathy.

However, treatment for drug addiction depends on different factors, such as the personality of the person, the perception of spirituality and religion, the history of diseases or illnesses of the person, and the availability of the programs that may be, or that are being offered.

Smoking

When it comes to smoking, the question arises why people smoke in the first place and when does it become an addiction?

There have been studies that the reason for smoking is purely psychological in nature. Blame it on movies, soap operas, and commercials on televisions - they try to glamorize smoking and make everyone feel at ease when you smoke. But once you try it, there are people who can never stop, and so this becomes an addiction, but the addiction to smoking nicotine can be fully stopped once you get to the psychological root of the problem. You first need to get to the core of the problem. Here are a couple of reasons why people are into nicotine.

- You want to feel glamorous and sophisticated in front of your friends.
- You don't want to feel left out by your friends who are all smoking.
- You want to feel independent.
- Your favorite actor or actress on television is smoking, so you want to be like them.
- You want to rebel against authority.
- You want to relax and take the stresses out of everyday life.

- You want to grow up, just a little too fast.

- You want to celebrate your anniversary or something grandiose that happened.

As you look at the reasons above, there is actually a pattern that evolves why you smoke - you are influenced by your peers, by your idols, or by television commercials, or televisions shows. But unfortunately, smoking is a form of addiction, and once you begin, it is extremely difficult to stop.

Strategy to Put Out the Cigarettes for Good

Just like drugs, once you start smoking, it's difficult to stop but it is possible to quit smoking. You just need a little bit of everything - a little bit of determination, guts, and willpower to finally end the addiction you have been desperately wanting to end for the longest time. Years in some cases.

There are several ways to quit smoking. One is to discover why you smoke in the first place and then try to deal with it by developing some kind of method or technique to stop smoking.

If you can't deal with it, get your friends to help you. The second would be to conquer your physical addiction to nicotine.

Here are a couple of suggestions that might get you off the ground and free you of your nicotine symptoms:

Determine what is really your motivation for quitting. Find out what your real reason is to want to quit smoking. Is it because you want to be free from nicotine addiction? or do you want to save some money? or get healthier? Whatever it is, try to assess yourself and find out why you want to quit smoking. In fact, quitting smoking helps you improve your life and gives you the greatest fulfillment - along with a greater sense of well-being for you and for your family. Take control of your life and don't let anyone or anything influence you in smoking.

Below are some motivations for quitting smoking.

Health Issues. Studies have proven again and again that smoking is bad for your health. It makes you sick with all kinds of diseases or illnesses which you have never heard of, but the most common one is cancer. Aside from these diseases, smoking also causes you to lose your sense of smell, gives you bad breath, and makes you lose your appetite, hence, losing weight. It also diminishes your energy.

Cosmetic Aspects. Cigarettes leave a very foul odor on the user and nicotine stains are usually all over their fingers. Aside from that, their teeth are mostly discolored (they sometimes turn bright yellow - good for your shirt but not for your teeth), and they make you age faster.

Relations with Others. There have been studies that state that second-hand smoking (breathing smoke exhaled by someone else who is smoking) is quite dangerous. Realizing that you are not only putting your own health in danger by smoking, but that of your loved ones can be a powerful motivation to help you to stop.

Finances. Because of smoking, you lose not only your priorities in life but your finances as well. You may spend far too much on cigarettes rather than those things that really matter. Save some money by stopping smoking and then save the money you save which leads ultimately to a richer life.

Determine the Psychological Issues. Another aid to quitting smoking is to try to determine the moments when you are most tempted to smoke. Is it when you want to relax, or when you are with a group of people who smoke? Try to focus on these moments and find something else to do at those times instead of smoking. You can also find ways to replace smoking with another form of activity as I mentioned earlier, such as doing a particular hobby, talking to your loved ones, or just going out and doing something new.

As much as possible, try to avoid mingling with people who are smoking, and with these people, avoid situations that make you want to smoke. Just remind yourself of the negative factors of smoking. Drink lots of water so that you will stay hydrated. Try to keep busy so that you can eventually forget about smoking.

Exercise, and take a deep breath when you feel like smoking. Ask your friends and family to help you quit smoking - create a support group through them.

Determine the Physical Addiction. Just like drugs, smoking is very addictive and the smoker might tend to have varying withdrawal symptoms whenever he suddenly stops smoking. He might feel irritable, uncomfortable, uneasy, suffer from headaches, chills, has trouble sleeping, or break out in a nervous sweat. But with different people come different techniques and methods of quitting. It depends on the person. Here are additional techniques to help you stop smoking:

Quitting "suddenly". There was a reality show on television a while ago called "Cold Turkey". The objective of the show was how to teach smokers to quit smoking through various challenges and means. Cold turkey means that you suddenly stop smoking altogether and without the least bit of preparation. However, the

disclaimer: *cold turkey is more effective for people who are not heavy smokers.*

When you go on a vacation or start a new hobby, make a definite resolution to yourself to stop smoking and this will be a lot easier for you since you are in a new environment and a new setting.

Gradually. Like any other kind of addiction, gradual withdrawal is the best response for some individuals. It starts slowly - from several cigarettes down to just one and then down to nothing at all.

Of course, you also need to take note of the time frame - when you expect to be down to two cigarettes a day - like a week or three days. During all of this time that you are gradually reducing your intake, just make sure that you are busy with something and involved in some hobbies or with your work. There are other and better things to do than smoking, such as spending time with your family or watching a movie!

Patches and Gums. There are those people who use nicotine patches and substitute cigarettes with gums. Nicotine patches take a few days before they take effect but with gum, it takes the sensation away almost immediately. These products actually help you in refusing the smell of cigarettes but it doesn't actually cure the addiction. They can help you treat the problem in two steps – first the habits associated with using cigarettes, and then the nicotine dependency, but since the nicotine dependency is the destructive part, and the patches and gums contain nicotine, you are not cured of your problem until you stop using them too.

Alcoholism

Just like smoking, there are several reasons why people drink. And most of them are already mentioned here, such as that it makes them more relaxed, it gives them more pleasure, friends or family members tend to influence them, they want to be part of the in-crowd, and also the major influence of liquor commercials on television and major broadcasts with known actors and actresses promoting them.

Strategy to Stop the Drinking Addiction

Alcoholism comes with a huge price. When people are under the influence of alcohol, they tend to be violent, and possibly cause harm to themselves and others. Aside from that, alcohol brings about sicknesses and illnesses such as liver cancer and other types of diseases.

Here are a few suggestions for dealing with alcoholism:

Determine the Psychological Issues. There is a reason why a person or yourself has started drinking heavily. To start, ask yourself these questions. Does it have something to do with your work? your career or with your family? Or is there a secret that you are keeping from others? Whatever it is, you have to get to the root of the problem because the problem is not just being addicted to alcohol - the deeper problem is the reason why you or another person in your life has resorted to such an option.

Once again, it may be too hard to go it alone, so again, get some help as your first step.

If the issue is with another person, try to get the person away from drinkers as much as possible and substitute drinking with other hobbies or interests. Instead of alcohol, ask this person to drink lots of water also or instead of.

Of course, I am referring to either helping someone else stop the drinking addiction or indeed yourself. Or both.

Gambling Addiction

Gambling is defined as an addiction that causes damage and harm to the gambler and others. This term is recognized in general as problem gambling or pathological gambling, which as some leading experts believe, even borders on mental illness.

Pathological gambling is characterized by each of the following attributes:

Lying. The gambler tries to hide this addiction by lying to his friends, family, and loved ones. And of course, to him or herself.

Withdrawal. Just as with drugs, alcohol, and cigarette addictions, behavioral patterns such as irritability, uneasiness, and discomfort surface when the addict suddenly ceases to gamble.

Escape. In many cases, gambling is a form of escape from the realities of life.

Need for excitement. The most important attribute of gambling - the gambler wagers more than he can handle so that he can feel the adrenaline pumping.

Loss of control. The gambler loses his self-control and keeps on gambling despite his willingness to stop.

Acts that are illegal. When families, friends fail to support the gambler, he then may resort to illegal acts such as embezzlement, robbery, or another type of thievery.

Some say that there is a biological basis to gambling and that gambling addiction is quite similar to chemical addiction in that pathological gamblers have much lower hormonal levels of norepinephrine than normal gamblers, who are not addicted.

Norepinephrine is a hormone that is secreted under stress, excitement and thrills so what gamblers do, is gamble to bring that hormone level up. There have also been studies that show that gamblers who lack the hormone serotonin also give in to this temptation.

Pathological gambling is also similar to other kinds of compulsive behaviors such as being pyromaniac, and kleptomaniac. It may also, be related to other disorders such as schizophrenia and antisocial personality disorder.

And there are similarities among these compulsive behaviors as to their primary cause - usually abuse in the home and other personal relationships. When there is abuse, it can often lead to compulsive behaviors such as gambling.

Strategy in treating the Gambling Addiction

There is hope for people who indulge in this form of addiction. It can be counteracted by drugs such as SSRI paroxetine and an antagonist drug called nalmefene, which has been quite effective in curing gambling addiction.

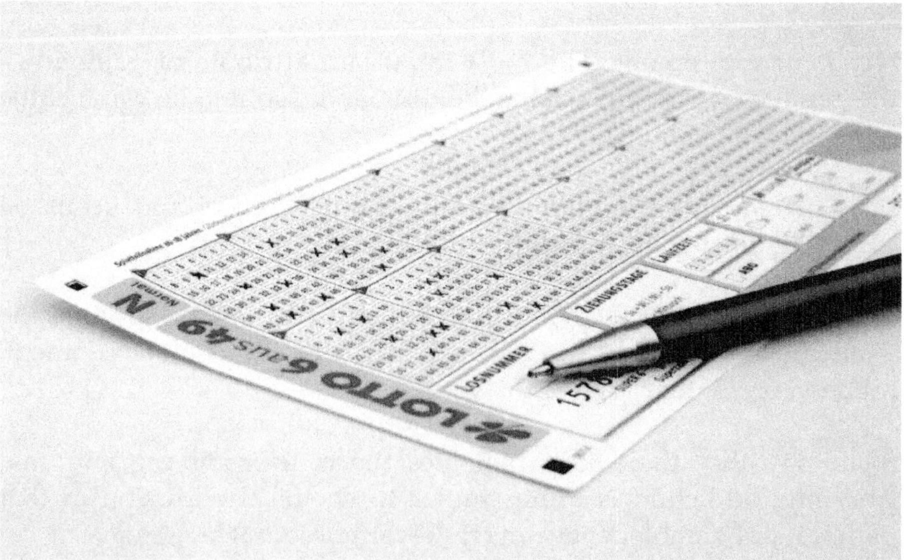

But there are also other treatments that don't involve drugs. Counseling is one, delivered by professional counselors, social workers, or psychologists. There are also other forms of treatment such as step-by-step programs, and among the famous ones is Gamblers Anonymous, which places much importance on peer and support groups.

Chapter Four: OTHER TYPES OF ADDICTIONS

It is also possible to be addicted to a normally harmless substance or activity. In this case, we can speak of addiction because the person is unreasonably dependent on the substance or activity and exhibits withdrawal symptoms similar to those of an addict when he does not have the substance he craves.

Some examples of these are:

Food Addiction

Food is obviously a very emotionally charged subject. We have associations in our minds relating to food that goes way back to childhood and infancy. We need food to live, so the way we deal with food can be an indication of our desire to live or lack of it. So, it's not surprising that food should often be the subject of some addictive behavior.

In fact, an article in the BBC News (January 30, 2003) claimed that fast foods are as addictive as heroin, and it might not be just journalistic hyperbole.

Addiction to specific foods

Sugar is one substance that has a drug-like effect on the brain and body. It increases the production of serotonin in the brain, which makes the person feel good - at least for a while until the effect wears off. This, in turn, creates a desire for more sugary and high-carbohydrate foods. People who have a tendency to depression are especially vulnerable to sugar cravings.

Fats also have an addictive effect, since they stimulate opoids or pleasure chemicals in the brain. A study of rats that were fed a high-fat diet showed that they had hormonal changes and no longer responded to the body's usual signals of satiety. In other words, they became addicted to fat and ate more and more of it.

Caffeine can also be addictive. We all know people who drink large amounts of coffee every day. Even a small daily amount can produce withdrawal symptoms - many people who indulge in caffeine experience headaches when they miss their morning coffee.

But we don't always remember that caffeine is added to soft drinks, especially colas, in amounts that have little to do with the difference in taste. It's no surprise, then, that Diet Coke is consumed in huge quantities daily by many people, who admit themselves that they are addicted to it.

Chocolate is another food that many people find difficult to resist. Not only does it contain sugar and fat, but also tryptophan, a precursor of serotonin, phenylethylamine, and anandamide, both neurotransmitters that increase the sensation of pleasure, and theobromine, a weaker relative of caffeine.

Cheese - even cheese contains opiates. Cows produce morphine naturally, some of which go into their milk. Cheese, being a more concentrated form of milk, contains a small but still detectable amount of morphine. In addition, milk, and therefore cheese too, contains casein, which, when digested, transforms into opiates called casomorphins.

Food Allergies - Paradoxically, allergies to certain foods cause a craving for them in some people instead of unpleasant symptoms that make them want to avoid them.

William Philpott, M.D., believes that in these people, contact with such food allergens triggers a rise in the brain of the opoid enkephalin, a narcotic and very addictive substance.

The most common food allergens are dairy products, wheat, coffee, eggs, and corn. The deeper problem here is that these foods, although craved by the allergic person, are still harmful to him, and can cause a variety of symptoms that are often difficult to trace back to an allergy to a certain food or foods. Some of these are arthritis, diabetes, migraines, asthma, obesity, and even schizophrenia.

Addiction to behaviors or activities

When a person is drawn to behavior that they can't control, this is also called a compulsion, and the line between compulsions and addictions is mostly a matter of vocabulary. The only difference is that an exterior physical substance is not usually involved in a compulsion. But since our own bodies produce pleasure-inducing substances, there is always something going on in the brain to explain why the activity is addictive.

Of course, the psychological aspect is just as important. An activity will become addictive to one person and not to another because of psychological factors: the tendency of the individual to some addictive behaviors in general, the significance of that particular activity to that person, and other things going on in their lives, such as stress, the state of their relationships and feelings of success or failure.

In fact, any activity can be considered addictive if it fulfills the same criteria as substance addictions: inability to control oneself, continued practice of the activity in the presence of harmful consequences, either physical or in one's personal or social life, extreme pleasure during the activity and withdrawal symptoms such as anxiety when the person is unable to practice their activity.

If you have a hobby that you love, even if you spend hours on it every week, as long as you manage to integrate it into your life in a harmonious way, it would be inaccurate to call it an addiction.

Many activities require sacrifice; if you want to get ahead in your job, you have to work much harder, if you want to win a sports competition, you have to train your body, and if you want to make beautiful music, you have to practice your instrument. And of course, all of these activities bring you great satisfaction when you succeed. They also include a positive intention or goal attached to the behavior which is controlled by the individual and not the other way around.

But when these activities are not addictions, there is a sense of freedom about indulging in them that is not present in the case of addiction. You do the activity by choice, and even though you might be devastated if you could no longer do it at all, stopping for a while because of other things in your life that need attention does not throw you into a state of deep anxiety. It's the difference between acting out of love and acting out of need. In fact, you can also be addicted to a person when your need for them outweighs your love for them.

The list of more general activities and behaviors that people can become addicted to is therefore endless. Some of the activities that are often cited as lending themselves to addictive behavior are:

Work - there is even a special word for these people: workaholics.

Extreme sports - they give an adrenaline rush.

Physical exercise - we've all heard of the runner's high.

Fiction - there is a large component here of escapism from the real world, as well as a vicarious adrenalin rush from watching or reading exciting stories.

Television - in combination with the escapism of watching fiction, there is also a hypnotic effect that comes from the flickering of the images on the screen in addition to a constant stream of images and sounds that can overwhelm the human brain, which was not really designed for such a steady barrage of sights and sounds.

Constant listening to music - as with television, the constant stream of sounds may become addictive. This might also reduce anxiety by distracting the person who does not wish to think about his problems.

Video games - Here we have excitement and an adrenaline rush, an escape from reality into an imaginary world, and a flickering hypnotic screen. What a combination!

Computers - This could include video games, different computer programs, surfing the Internet, participating in online forums and chats, or compulsively checking your email or social media every five minutes.

ADDICTION CONCLUSION

Be it any kind of addiction - drugs, alcohol, cigarettes, or gambling and other addictive behaviors, there is still hope for everyone. There is a solution to each of these problems. All that you need to do is to have the determination and the willpower to take on the challenge and fight them, and instill in your mind thoughts that you can overcome your problem.

The solution might not come overnight, but the important thing is your desire to help yourself in tackling all of the possible addictive problems you yourself, a friend, or a family member may currently be struggling with.

There is help, but the desire to be healed must come from you first before anyone else can help you with it. I personally believe that help or support although very important is just 5% of the solution. The other 95% is up to you and your participation in the activities that eliminate the addiction. Support is an invaluable element though so don't neglect it, it is YOU who has to do the work. - Over Time.

So, don't lose hope if you feel that you haven't overcome the problem yet. As with all kinds of addictions, determine the root cause of the problem and start from there. Also, plan your action and take some immediate action. And of course, give yourself a chance. Everyone needs a second chance, especially those who have addiction problems.

By following these simple strategies in this book, eventually, you will discover that your addiction is slowly fading, and when you overcome it, your peace of mind and satisfaction will be more gratifying than the fundamentally false pleasure that you formerly derived from your addiction.

Thanks for Listening

Andy Raingold.

ELIMINATE THE NEGATIVES SERIES

ELIMINATE THE NEGATIVES

THE FIRST STEPS TO LIVING
A BETTER LIFE EXPERIENCE.

Written By:
Andy Raingold

Graphic Design By: Stephen Hawkins.
Special Thanks to Nathanial Dasco & Ikhide Oshoma

ELIMINATE THE NEGATIVES PREFACE:

The book you now hold in your hands is both a practical workshop to take you closer to the success in life that you seek, and, an introduction to more of the titles in this series and in particular a set of 3 programs I will make available to you the serious success seeker.

You see, any single book cannot or will not turn you into the success that you seek to become. But each will move you one step closer, within a specific area to that which you seek. In our case, eliminating The Negatives

From a simple comment passed to you on the street by a stranger to the world's greatest workbooks and literature, you will move a step closer to your end goal if you recognize the wisdom being passed on to you through the aforementioned as well as other information passed through various modern media types, even if the step is a tiny or perhaps even a minuscule move closer to your end goal or result. Each will eventually help and guide you towards your chosen end.

However, with the right guidance, you can more swiftly be taken much closer, if not directly to success through the knowledge that you discover along your journey. Or rather, the application of that knowledge and your integrated thoughts, actions, and behaviors.

But be warned, what I just wrote does not include a completely fully integrated analysis of the subject or what you might call a "quote" that will lead you where you want to go in life. I say that because earlier I mentioned that this was an introduction to other titles and programs that I have made available to you as well as this workbook. The workbook you now hold contains the vital first step in a process that will move you much closer to your end goal just so long as you put in the required effort to do so after recognizing the value contained herein.

We will soon move into the first section of this little book but first, let me tell you why I have taken this route and briefly introduce you to the process.

First, I have presented the information as it is here because the knowledge required for success in anything cannot be imparted through a single book on one general subject. That is unless the book was 100,000 pages or more long. To that end and to remove a good many of the pages of that vast archive I have decided to pass on this knowledge through a series of short books called The Assertive Life Series, Eliminate The Negatives, and other series by Andy Raingold. This is essentially to cover as much ground as possible required for the foundation of knowledge that you will need, as well as three main programs that although not necessary will greatly enhance the possibility of success for you.

As suggested, you may wish to go it alone and study each of the short books alone or you may wish to take the programs that will get you there with greater understanding and possibly much faster with even greater success as a result. That decision is entirely up to you and although I recommend that you take the full programs, that is by no means mandatory as you will still take one or more steps closer to the success you seek by going it alone and following the instruction within this short book. That said, many of these short collections were designed as a program or collection of workshops in and of themselves.

You can see the additional titles at the back of this and other Assertive Life Series books but there is a three-step process that I want to mention to make sure you get why I have taken this approach and so that you know the full impact of the programs.

The programs are titled:

Success Redefined - Available as paperback or kindle only. This is a preliminary introduction to the three main programs which are:

Success Beyond Purpose - Legacy and purpose.
Success Powerfunnels - Goals and productivity.
Success Beyond Mindset - Going beyond mindset.

Each includes a free introductory title as indicated below.

First Level: Mastering Your Destiny
Second Level: Your Seven Step Goal Setting Workshop
Third Level: 5 Ways to Develop A Mindset for Success

The above three program levels of success and free introduction titles each deal with a specific subject area as suggested above and are accessible through the download resource at the back of this book.

You will not have heard most of this information anywhere else as I spent a lifetime developing them and putting them together after many and varied tests and much study.

As mentioned previously, you can move through your own success journey any route you choose but I highly recommend moving from the point of Eliminating The Negatives, then into the "Success Beyond Purpose" process into "Success Powerfunnels" and finally, "Success Beyond Purpose". You may choose either the book or program version.

And again, as previously suggested these cover Purpose, Goals and Productivity (getting vast amounts of work done fast), and Mindset. But all approaches are completely new and not available elsewhere as far as I know.

But for now, let us continue to create greater success in our lives by taking the first step by "Eliminating The Negatives" in preparations for greater possibilities that lie just around the corner. The second section is where the workshop part of this book begins but we need to cover some basic principles to prepare the ground.

And please remember you do not have to buy any other program in order to become successful. I just thought that it would be a good idea to place some steps before you in order to give you an idea of the route you will most likely need to take on your success journey. Whether you do that alone, or through the books and programs of other authors and program creators, or the ones I provide, or indeed, a mix of both. The choice is and always has been yours. All that is now left to say is enjoy the journey and be kind to yourself as you begin to Eliminate The Negatives.

SECTION 1:

Transform Negativity

Developing a General Positive Outlook

ELIMINATE THE NEGATIVES INTRODUCTION

If we choose the route to attempt to transform negatives into positives then changing perspective will nearly always help us to see things from another angle. Enabling us to be able to weigh the possibilities that our new situation may offer us when we are considering the transformation of the negative into the positive.

Transforming the negative into the positive is not a simple matter of taking a day or a specific moment to transform ourselves but a daily exercise that we must learn to carry with us for our well-being. We can however make great headway by employing the workshop content beginning in section 2 of this book where we will begin to take a different approach from transformation.

Negativity can become a bad habit if we don't get used to keeping a healthy perspective. For this reason, sometimes, our attitude can make situations worse, and in many cases, more than the initial problems themselves.

In this first section of the book, you now hold we will reveal some keys to transforming the negative into positive in a realistic way. Once you put them into practice, you will not only begin to feel better, but you will get better at dealing with situations that may arise along the way. And of course, you will in most cases begin to get better results from your actions in life.

However, this first section is really an introduction if you will to the second section where we begin to dig deep into Eliminating the Negatives in your life. But first, let's take a birds-eye view of positive and negative in more general terms.

Part One:
What Is Negativity? What is positivity?

Negativity

Negativity is a prevalent mental state in people; although it cannot be continually maintained without something to hold on to, it is nevertheless a widespread state.

The point is that very little is needed for the mind to focus on the negative; by our nature, we can clearly see a hostile or negative act present in the thousands of right actions that make up a person's whole life or see the negative repercussion of some past situation in our present life even though in most part we are being positive. There's a reason for that which we will go into in the second section of this book.

On many occasions, negative causes are attributed to a person's particular behavior; for example, a lover may have hundreds of good qualities that should fill us with happiness with their mere presence. However, sometimes a simple act of forgetfulness such as forgetting your girlfriend's birthday can serve to bring an abrupt end to the relationship in a worst-case scenario.

Another example is when a child who may have displayed many positive thoughts and actions towards his parents commits a single act of rebellion which shows the child to be ungrateful, or worse still.

Sometimes our mind may turn and change thousands of times and use thousands of axioms to justify its Negativity; it was that person or that other person; thus, the climbing plant of Negativity requires a substrate on which to stay or cling to. All this can lead us to a very bitter place of resentment, which is not really a recommended state to be in.

What Is Positivity?

Positivity is not the tendency to believe that "positive thinking" really works to make relevant changes in the medium to long term. As we will see today, positivity means much more than merely trying to think and say positive things even when you don't hear them yourself. Today we discover instead what positivity is and how it can change us from the foundations up.

Positivity is the totality of positive emotions that the human body can feel and their consequences on human psychophysiology. We can then begin to glimpse the real value of our emotions and understand how they can interact with our daily life.

Strategies to Turn Negativity into positivity

Turn your thoughts into relative thoughts.

Imagine that you have written to your best friend and that he has seen the message, but he has not replied. Suddenly, questions start to appear in your mind about whether he is angry with you if you have said something that could have made him feel bad.

What is happening is then in error? And perhaps nothing that is occurring to you is accurate at all. It's not reality-based at all.

Your friend may be busy, his battery may have run out just when he saw your message, and a thousand other things may have happened. So do not take your thoughts as an absolute truth because they are significantly influenced by the feelings that are approaching you at that moment in response to what is currently happening.

How true are your thoughts? Ask yourself with your logical mind, and you will see how you begin to see everything more clearly.

Reverse reality

A very curious and fun technique to transform a negative into a positive is to reverse what is happening to you. For example, instead of starting the day with "how bad I feel," propose and say to yourself: "Today I am going to feel good." Of course, you should try to put everything into actually feeling and believing it, and then achieving it becomes much easier at the same time.

Repeat it as many times as necessary until you internalize the thought and know that it is much better to propose to yourself that all is well, and then to take advantage of the day than to spend it somewhere between complaints and pessimism. You have the power to change the way you see and experience things.

In the face of the negative, always have a positive answer.

We cannot control everything that happens to us. Tomorrow we may be fired from our work, we may not be able to pay for the apartment, or our partner may leave us.

However, the worst we can do is complain, immerse ourselves in victimhood, feed that Negativity surrounding us, and make it much more robust. How can we avoid this? By responding to adversity with positivity. This is the basis of positive thinking and we will take a deeper look into it in section 2, and we may come to eliminate it altogether. But for now, let's say that responding to negative situations in a positive way is the way to go.

For example, in the face of a possible job layoff, we can take a different approach and say to ourselves: "This is a great opportunity to find another job that helps me grow even more." Or in the aftermath of a breakup, we can say to ourselves: "now I will be able to dedicate much more time and discover what I want in a future relationship."

Practice mindfulness!

Mindfulness is a practice that can help you be much more positive because one of its main features is inviting you to focus on the present moment, stop living in the past, and worry about the future. In other words, it focuses on the "here and now." In a positive life-affirming way.

With regular practice (either formally or informally), you will learn to see your thoughts without judging them, making the most of the variations and the good they may have. You will also realize that many of us are conditioned by what we feel and how this prevents us from seeing how much we can learn from some of the situations we experience. Above all, life is about having and learning from new experiences that help us to grow.

Love yourself and give yourself a lot of pampering

We couldn't finish these basic strategies on turning negative into positive without mentioning how important it is to love and pamper ourselves. If we don't do this, it will be almost impossible for us to see something positive in the sometimes negative things that happen to us.

We always tend to interpret whether something is right or wrong based on how other people approve of our behavior or not. Also, we may even leave our well-being in the hands of others. Please see Upgrade Your Happiness - Six Steps To Greater Joy, Success, and a Truly Fulfilling Life for changing this unsavory predicament.

We must learn to prioritize ourselves, to give ourselves the value we deserve without anyone having to tell us, to love ourselves without anyone coming to declare how much they love us.

It is time to take charge of life and discover that the negative is just a matter of perspective. Didn't you always think that making a mistake meant failure, only to realize later that it meant opportunity? Let us not fall into victimization, nor suffer in vain. Life is much simpler than we think, only that sometimes our thoughts, guided by our emotions, play tricks on us, turn into remnants and cancel us out. If we allow them to.

Part Two:
How Do You Like Your Life So Far?

The Need To Examine Your Life

"*A life without examination isn't worth living*" is the conclusion that Socrates uses to justify his teaching methods. This appeals above all to the importance of examining oneself and others to maintain a critical attitude about our actions and about our lives with the ultimate goal of evolving to be the most unique person we can be.

In the dialogues before the court of Athens, Socrates develops the argument that he does not deserve death, since he intends to do good by trying to convince each one through maieutics, irony, and dialogues, that Instead of worrying about the things that most people worry about, they should worry about being the best and the most sensible person they can be.

The phrase "*A life without examination is not worth living*" is found near the end of the Apology of Socrates in paragraph 38a, where he appeals that he does not deserve the death penalty for trying to convince others to follow his example to abandon what most people worry about: businesses, family finances, military commanders, speeches in assemblies, magistrates, alliances and party struggles.

The introduction to the phrase "*a life without examination is not worth living*" is Socrates' argument about what it deserves. One of the options he suggests is maintenance at the Pritaneo. In Pritaneo, the benefactors of the city received the honor of being fed. Since Socrates considered his action to be a greater good then, perhaps, he deserved this honor.

To avoid the death penalty, Socrates affirms that he knows that he must suggest evil or punishment that he knows is bad for him, such as prison (where he argues that he does not deserve to live as a slave of the magistrates); a fine (but he claims he has no money) or banishment.

When Socrates argues about the possibility of punishing himself with exile, or according to how the Athenians see it: living far away in silence leading a quiet life, he affirms that it is difficult to persuade those present that for him this means disobeying God because the greatest good is talking, to examine oneself, and others because *"a life without examination is not worth living."*

"If I say that the greatest good for a man is precisely this, to have conversations every day about virtue and the other subjects that you have heard me talk about when I examined myself and others, and if I say that a life without examination has no purpose in living it for man, you will believe me even less. "

Other phrases of the philosopher Socrates are:

"The true wisdom is in recognizing your own ignorance."
"It is better to suffer an injustice than to commit it."
"Pride separates people, humility unites them.

Moving on…

Do You Have Regrets?

What would you have done if you believed you could do anything, and not just what life and authority placed before you?

In this time of balance, it is inevitable to remember the good, the bad, and the ugly things that we live with during the years. Achievements achieved, dreams fulfilled, mistakes, and events that positively or negatively impacted our lives. Likewise, our past comes to light in all its splendor; and sometimes, you will miss something of it. You would instead not start doing this exercise and leave the memories in that trunk with locks and never open it. However, it is in these moments that we unintentionally remember that we could have done things differently.

Regret is defined as the regret that a person feels for something they have said, done, or not done. The most common regrets are related to health, love, and living in the present. You have to ask yourself that question, regardless of age, what do you regret in your life?

Within each area of your life.

What to do when you regret something

Sometimes, you feel that your life is not what you expected. You looked different on a personal, professional, or even family level; you consider that the decisions you made were not the best. Or, on the contrary, you think that although you are not in the best place, you learned from all this and are enjoying the results to the fullest right now.

Most people feel uneasy about their present; they remember their past and long for a future that does not exist due to fears and beliefs that prevented their past projects from ever becoming manifest.

Evaluate if these thoughts of dissatisfaction have to do with plans or projects that other people generalize, that is, evaluate if what you long for are your dreams and your goals or belong more to scripts or programs created by family or society in general. A simple example is a script that the vast majority of people execute: study, look for a job, go into debt, get married, have a family, go to a job they hate every day for the rest of their life, etc. We will look at this again, later in section 3.

If you look at it, it seems that the vast majority follow this pattern, but it is not clear if it is what they really dreamed of or whether they just followed the script given them by society and authority.

Remember that we have one life, and the aim is to enjoy it, not to live others' lives, but yours with successes, mistakes, failures, and learnings all of your own making. The important thing is to be clear that you were the one responsible and so only you can change it. So, take charge of your life knowing that nobody, absolutely nobody, can tell you what to do with it.

So, if you regret where you are today, assume your responsibility, evaluate what is within your power to change, and then do it, and do not wait for the perfect moment to arrive, instead, make it happen. Study, travel, work, undertake, love, whatever needs to be done, do it. If you are afraid, be afraid also. The valuable thing about realizing that you stopped doing and regretting it is that you still have time to execute it. You can always change your present and your future and, in this way, regain control of your life.

Is change possible? You can live a better life.

As I just iterated, change is absolutely possible if we aim towards what we want and work to bring it about. (this is the purpose of the www.successbeyondpurpose.com website. Knowing what you really want). That site also helps solve common success blockers such as a lack of general motivation and overwhelm that is also covered in the Success Redefined book.

Although we are mostly not aware of it, our body is continually changing. Approximately every seven years, all the cells in our body are renewed and replaced in an unstoppable transformation process.

As far as we can affirm then, change is inherent to the human being. We change permanently; however, we are much more reluctant to incorporate effective changes in our lives regarding our personality and behavior.

How can we change?

Transformation is possible as long as we have a firm conviction and a high dose of desire to make the desired changes. It is not easy; it requires immersing yourself in a process that involves self-observation to detect those behaviors or characteristics we do not feel comfortable having within our personality. This leads us to develop a high degree of self-knowledge that facilitates self-regulation to consolidate the desired changes.

This process involves training, gymnastics for the brain in which the role of the psychotherapist is fundamental. It is widespread to take as valid the collaboration, for example of a personal trainer, that helps us keep our body in shape, but when it comes to changing aspects of our personality, we suppose that we can achieve it alone, and to a certain degree it is possible. Still, with a professional's help, the path will always be much more direct than when we try to change by ourselves. Let us now know how our personality is composed and the traits that we can modify from it:

- **Received Personality**: Is genetically conditioned, and it is our basic temperament. It cannot be modified.
- **Learned personality**: Is the set of affective, cognitive, and operational skills we possess. Our character.
- **Chosen personality**: Represented by our character and behavior in the situations that arise.

The learned personality is the most important when deciding to change; it is the one that we can influence if we want to improve.

So, you can do a "reset" and modify those mechanisms that do not reflect or favor a good quality of life.

To make the representation of change more graphic, we could interpret our brain alongside computing. Our brain would come to operate thanks to overly complicated software, represented by our entire belief system. At one point, we had the latest version of that software, but over time it lost its validity, hence the need to perform a "reset" or update our operating system that lives by the old rules, situations, and beliefs that no longer serve us. We will dig into the practical process involved in section two.

Psychotherapy helps us to train our minds to achieve better and more ecological and sustainable management of our emotions. In the long term, it enables us to change into a form that favors a better quality of life and better reflects our own preferences.

Getting to know yourself

Knowing oneself is essential in aspiring to the level of happiness we seek to achieve. This distinction is made because we talk about happiness, and it is sold to us as a state of absolute well-being, in which our projects are fulfilled, in which everything turns out to a specific order. And that is a utopia with little sense and is mostly result-based. There are constant changes in life that we cannot control, and aspiring for everything to go as we want is to fall into a dangerous trap since we have a tendency to allow our general well-being dependent on uncontrollable external factors. Please see my book, "Upgrade Your Happiness" for more detailed instruction on achieving greater happiness in life.

The happiness of self-knowledge has other nuances, as we are learning to assume that not everything will be perfect. What's more, the first thing we believe is that each of us has his or her own shadows, and that's okay too. We cannot have light without having shades of darkness also. There are many ways to access self-knowledge, but I find a particularly useful and valid system is provided by the Enneagram. Of course, run with a helpful guide and with some common sense. As in everything, our society tends to simplify, categorize, and see how returns can be made on anything that appears to be valid. But with the premise of its fair use, the Enneagram can help a lot.

It can help for several reasons. You can see what your "false personality" or "neurotic personality" is and realize that it is like that of many others who are in your same category (in the language of the Enneagram, who have the same enneatype).

Realizing that you are not as original as you thought is a sound dose of humility, but at the same time, it can be liberating. And also, seeing those behavior patterns helps you detect when you are there. And knowing that you are there neurotically can hurt a bit at first, but then it allows you to decide (or begin to decide) when you don't want to be there, trapped by your supposed programming.

Because what truly makes us unique is under those layers of personality. We will always have a "personality," an individual "enneatype." But what connects us with ourselves is under those layers, and discovering it, contacting that, with what we call essence, changes everything. It is however a slow process; you have to work on it. There are advances and setbacks, but being on that path allows you to connect with something real in yourself. Something that does not depend on anything external. Something stable in itself. And although there may be times when you want to throw in the towel, being there is the closest thing to heightened happiness and love. And I speak of happiness with capital letters, not of the euphoria of sporadic triumphs or success. And of real Love, not of possible substitutes.

It is difficult to convey all this in words. To explain the magic of knowing yourself with the limitations of language, you have to live it and experience it. Also, nobody is there to assure you that by being on a particular path, you will achieve what I am speaking of. Many abandon the search, those who get tired or are scared or impatient - those who fear discovering something horrible about themselves. But the effort made in the right direction is always worth it because no matter where you find yourself right now, you will return transformed. Just a warning, if you go down that road, you will discover that the real aim is to get out of your comfort zone and into action.

Positive thinking should be realistic, focused on the real facts, seeking solutions, making decisions, being practical, being useful, and having a more objective and scientific thought process. It is not easy to have the serenity of mind and vision to see what is happening in your life and to then mobilize yourself exclusively to solve everything you can, and it is not easy to be practical in times of difficulty or conflict.

Many people give free rein to the emotional charge that they experience; they are carried away by impressions, assumptions, value judgments, hunches, suspicions, fears, anger, sympathies. That distorts reality. They do not see what happens but what appears to them to have occurred. They interpret reality from the emotional charge, but emotions distort the facts. They do not see clearly and transparently but through their perspective or focus. The negative thought then interprets and distorts reality, makes it more difficult, and becomes a subjective thought, guided by the emotional burden, and creates discomfort, and then moves the individual away from solutions and basic effectiveness.

How you face reality and act on a negative dramatically impacts your ability to resolve self-esteem issues, and more general and emotional well-being states.

Positive people are more optimistic, confident, determined, and enterprising; they seem to enjoy more than what life may actually have in store for them. Negative people tend to suffer or at the very least suffer more than necessary; they do not seem to fully enjoy their lives even if they have reasons to do so.

Why a style of thought or way of thinking?

The way of thinking does not refer to beliefs, values, philosophy of life. Each person is free to think as he likes; each decides what to believe, with what ideology and philosophy of life to identify. Usually developed over a long period. The cognitive style or way of thinking refers to our thinking behavior, and to the thought mechanisms used regularly, to thinking habits, specifically to a kind of internal dialogue or internalized speech.

How do you talk to yourself? What do you talk about? How long do you talk to yourself? What does your inner address pursue? Do you tend to act or ruminate on matters? Are you able to stop that internal dialogue? Do you know how to find silence, and to stop thinking? What emotions activate your inner dialogue?

The style of thought or way of thinking has to do with the personality pattern or practice of being and with the learning carried out from strong role models at an early age. People are not born positive or negative, practical and happy, or worried and distressed. The personality pattern we have has more to do with some essential personality traits that go into our genetic code; it is a predisposition that is engraved in our central nervous system.

Children show massive differences, even between siblings. Some people are introverts, while others are extroverts, some are calm and confident and others may be shy, reflective and impulsive, rigid and flexible. What are your most prominent character traits?

Personality traits are shaped by learning, enhancing, or other nuances. The knowledge produced by observation and imitation from the parents' behavior is compelling in developing character or personality. Early experience has a significant impact on the development of the personality traits that the genetic code carries. Each person tends to identify more with their father or mother in terms of character traits, personality, or way of being.

It becomes surprising just how cognitive styles resemble that of either parent. Who are you more like in the way you think or take things that happen to you, your father or your mother?

Do you know the reason for your discomfort? Perhaps it is within yourself?

What occurs inside our head has a direct emotional translation.

Tell me how you think, and I'll tell you how you feel. If you repeatedly ruminate on concerns, doubts, fears, difficulties, or memories, there's a good chance your feelings will reflect those thoughts. On the other hand, if you focus on what you do, you live within the five senses, reflect just enough to make good decisions, act decisively, stop to savor the small but pleasant moments, and feel a sense of general well-being you will most likely get much closer to the state they call happiness.

There are ways of thinking that cause pain and lead to difficulties or problems. On a physical level, we usually identify risks, what is not healthy, and avoid them. On an emotional level, we are more ignorant and do not perceive the risks as well. Just as putting your hand in the fire burns, ruminating negative concerns regularly can cause some anguish at best.

It is necessary then to begin the process to identify those harmful cognitive mechanisms, ways of thinking, or thinking actions that generate discomfort and cause us to get ourselves into difficulties. There is no point in doing what makes or feels terrible, only out of habit or not knowing how to do things in more beneficial ways. We must learn to take care of our emotional health.

These are some ways of thinking and beliefs people adopt that stop them from finding fault in themselves:

Recurring concerns

Some people are excessively reflective. They think continuously, their head does not stop thinking, they talk regularly, do not get enough rest, and hardly make time for themselves to enjoy a specific activity such as cinema, dancing, reading, crafts, and so on. Thinking continuously, living in an endless rumination on normal everyday matters, making others' problems your own, and worrying about them more than the person concerned, are cognitive habits that are exhausting, drain a lot of energy, and generate emotional discomfort.

Anticipate difficulties

Putting excessive enthusiasm into thinking or believing that everything works as planned, that nothing arises to alter it, leads to identifying many difficulties that may never occur at all. How many times have you felt that you have suffered unnecessarily, fearing situations that later did not happen? You were convinced that you were going to fail an exam, and then you passed it. You were afraid of a reprimand that was never given. You go to a meeting where your boss summons you fearing what he might say to you, and then it turned out to be a minor exchange of views or ideas. You cannot suffer without reasons existing or before an incident occurs if it ever does unless you allow yourself to go through that suffering.

Confusing possible and probable

Living any possibility as highly probable is a cognitive error. The belief of something happening does not mean that it will happen at all. You have to use reason when thinking about the probability that something can happen, and so it does not mean that it will happen. For example, an accident and/or sudden death. Is it possible to have a traffic accident? Is it probable? Logically, all drivers are exposed to the possibility of a traffic accident on a daily basis. The question is: are you likely to have a traffic accident? If you are responsible, and operate within the controlled speed limits, respect the road rules, and are respectful of other drivers, the probability of having an accident is very low. Is it possible to die by sudden death? Sure. But is it probable? The degree of probability will depend on a person's age and state of health.

We must know and come to terms with the possibility of a variety of unpleasant or traumatic situations happening, but we must also identify and manage our behavior based on the degree of probability of some unfortunate accident ever happening.

Getting carried away by mental impressions, intuition, suspicion

"I'm afraid," "I suspect this," "I suspect that," "I'm afraid that so and so is not being honest, that he is going to play me." These kinds of statements that may occur in one's internal dialogue determine behavior. They influence how a personal relationship is established, on the defensive, suspicious, keeping a distance, observing what confirms previous suspicions. Logically, with these kinds of impressions, assumptions, or past judgments, there is little to no possibility of ever developing a cordial relationship.

From the Theory of a Self-fulfilling Prophecy, it is explained how suspicions end up being fulfilled. When you fear that something will happen, you organize your behavior, without being aware of it, to make sure that the prophecy ends up happening; you do everything that needs to be done so that the fear ends up being fulfilled, it becomes a reality. "You see? I already told you," and so on. People who are carried away by impressions are almost always right, not because of their ability to read the future but because of their ability in making their suspicions come true.

Unleashing suspicions, "think negatively and you'll be right."

Suspicious people suffer a lot and may even end up alone. They are victims of their own paranoid thoughts. They always find someone in their family, work, or n some social context to be held responsible for all their ills. They have no sense of self-criticism; they live convinced that there are people who seek to cause them evil. "Think wrong and you will be right" is a way of relating to the world. They are distrustful people. They are those that one day tells you, "you told me, and you don't even remember it". They are observant, thoughtful, detailed, of who live in their world and tend to perceive or interpret reality in the way of betrayal or "I can't trust myself."

These people bear the penalty for their behavior; they suffer and generate disaffection.

It is fashionable to build conspiracy theories about factual powers that move the world, in which people are just puppets of those managed by those powers.

These beliefs are a form of rejection of socially established and generate intellectual or cultural marginality.

Focusing your attention on the "bad."

Some live focused on the "bad," with the attention focus on detecting what they do not like, annoys, or annoys them, does not seem fair, or is not correct... It is like living in a forest, standing in front of the trunk of a tree, and thinking, what forest is this that only has one tree? If you move only a meter away and take a broader perspective, you see reality; it is a forest full of trees. The truth is polychrome; it is not monochrome. There is everything: good, bad, attractive, objectionable, satisfactory, and unpleasant. It makes no sense to focus attention on one aspect because reality seems to be distorted, then perceiving it in a biased way and then suffering the consequences.

Fear of being wrong

Error is part of the total human condition; it is an element of the learning process. While learning, it is customary to often make mistakes and then rectify those mistakes. People are not machines. Even when a behavior has already been discovered and consolidated, it is easy for errors to continue being made due to distraction, absent-mindedness, excess responsibility, and such.

Not understanding or tolerating the mistake multiplies the fear of being wrong. Understanding the possibility of error increases confidence and courage in the execution of any task. Here we must return to the previous argument. The possibility of error exists and will always exist. We must know how to live with it; the probability of error is in our hands and will depend on the level of preparation, concentration, and confidence we input. We can reduce the likelihood of being wrong, but we cannot ignore the possibility of it ever happening.

Perfectionism

Aspiring to excellence should not be confused with the need to be excellent at all times and in any task you perform. Perfectionism is a mechanism that reduces efficiency in study, limits self-confidence, and generates anguish and dissatisfaction in general. Perfectionists are slow, too orderly, linear, controlling, and indecisive; they need everything to align to achieve perfection. There is a lot of attention to detail, doubts, and endless revisions behind this attitude, making sure that it is correct, and almost always leading to errors. The perfectionist ends the exam soon because he has prepared for it but does not tend to deliver it; he reviews it over and over again, doubts the answers noted down, checks them, doubts and changes them, wants to make sure before handing it in, feels distressed and ends up committing mistakes for their perfectionism. Also, perfectionism makes you unable to work in a team. The perfectionist needs to do it himself, as he sees it and how he would do it, inhibits the other team members' initiative, makes objections one after another, does not delegate, slows down the work process, and generates conflicts. The perfectionist is unbearable and is an obstacle to teamwork.

Affirmations such as “would” or “should.”

When the internal dialogue contains "should" or "would have," the thought transfers a fundamental expectation, which you do not feel capable of achieving. Still, you cannot forgive yourself for not achieving it. "I should quit smoking" assumes that you are aware of the negative consequences of smoking but that you do not feel capable of doing so, and you will then most likely not succeed. "It should be calmer" conveys that a person feels unable to remain calm and control his or her character. When the internal dialogue contemplates statements such as "I am going to," the will, determination, and decision to do so is much stronger than with the word "should." "I'm going to" affirms that you will be taking the step, often followed by actually doing it.

Affirmations such as “what if? “

It is quite common to look back and think, "what if…?" this, that or the other. This self-talk is common after an accident or misfortune of some kind. And, "What if I had called? What if I had noticed? What if he had accepted the proposal? What if I hadn't said that?" and so on.

Going back is impossible; what has been done is already done; you cannot change what has already happened. Going back and asking yourself questions that don't get an answer is absurd and causes much discomfort. It is unprovable that going around again, something impossible to predict would have turned out otherwise. Making these kinds of claims is an ineffective and discomforting exercise.

Affirmations with "..., but ..."

"We are fine, fortunately, but we don't know what could have happened in a particular situation."

"But" is used a lot to suppress satisfaction, to set limits on recreation and enjoyment. It is a statement that represses joy, happiness, recognition, or pleasure; it is like enjoying in half measures. Our society knows how to reprimand, correct, point out defects; it costs much more to praise, recognize, and identify the good. In this culture of the negative, "but" represents a brake on really remembering the good and thoroughly enjoying the satisfaction that comes with it.

Statements such as: "It's not fair..."

Some people set themselves up as harsh judges and often verbalize "it's not fair" in their internal dialogue. This statement identifies rigid people on a cognitive level, unwilling to redirect their perspective, and with little relative sense of opinions. They do not understand that there are different views and that the truth can be close according to context, customs, beliefs, and culture. There is no code of justice behind the decisions, but people who doubt and make logical decisions more or less arbitrary. You can agree, or disagree, but all behavior responds to a logic that must be known and understood, even if it is to be disputed. It makes no sense "is or is not fair." It supposes a not very tolerant, frustration-filled, self-centered thought, which usually generates more frustration. It is an immature way of thinking, a bit adolescent if you will.

Avoiding anxiety-inducing situations

A reasonably common mechanism is to flee or avoid situations that generate anxiety. Some people simply choose to live trying to escape difficulties, problems, and conflicts. That flight option often makes them vulnerable. Fears are fed into fears through escape or avoidance behaviors. Those who avoid difficulty, conflict, and fear reinforce their limited competence to manage them and are progressively more vulnerable to them.

Getting defensive, not listening.

Getting defensive, not listening, and counterattacking is common and is a misguided strategy. It tends to generate emotional distance, blocks communication, and multiplies interpersonal conflicts. Those who practice this strategy do not suffer, but they are left alone. Emotional discomfort comes to them in the medium and long term, when they realize that everyone has abandoned them.

Imposing your point of view or pretending to be right

If it's logical to be wrong, the logical thing is to accept the mistake and apologize if appropriate. It is a very wrong tactic to be stubborn, argue, and try to be right above all else. The more stubborn one is to hide or justify the error, the more mistaken the error is.

Lack of empathy, pride

It's surprising how little empathy many people show. They are those who do not perceive that they tire in their conversations, run over in their opinions, bore in their stories, and attack in their postulates. They are people who run over their interlocutors without being aware of it. Since they don't realize it, they hardly ever suffer from it.

Jealousy

Possessive love is not loving at all. Possessive love is a distrustful, irrational, emasculating type of love that restricts freedom. It is a form of suspicion or mistrust. Some confuse "a lot of love" with jealousy as a source of problems for jealousy and those who suffer from envy. It is a mechanism that generates a lot of anguish in the jealous person and produces satiety in those who suffer from jealousy. Jealousy is the shortest and most direct way to break up any relationship.

Envy, irrational competition

Some live more aware of the lives of others than of their own lives. They try to live the lives of others. What they are and what they have is not enough for them. They need to surpass others, be more or have more than their environment allows. They are envious and competitive people. They practice insane, dishonest, and unfair competitive tactics. They tend to criticize and disqualify; they do not value or rejoice in the successes of others. This cognitive mechanism also generates a lot of discomforts and social rejection. Those who function like this are survivors; they try to pretend, compete permanently and are socially rejected.

Egocentrism, wanting to have a leading role or be a protagonist

We all know the one who wants to be the child at the christening, the groom at the wedding, and the dead at the funeral, always wants to be the protagonist. He speaks, intervenes, participates, and takes the floor without much content to offer. Why does he do this? Well, because he needs to. He cannot stand to go unnoticed; he needs to have and feel a leading role; he needs to be the center of attention. He always tries to "hit the mark," give the most consistent opinion and tell the funniest joke. He doesn't worry about how to get the prominence he needs to feel like somebody. His desire to take center stage is directly proportional to the disaffection he generates in others.

Avoiding dealing with problems

"From problems, it is better to run away" is a philosophy of life. As problems generate imbalance, uncertainty, discomfort, it seems that it is better to avoid them. These people think that "problems are solved by default," that is, by doing nothing. Running away from the problem makes the conflict situation latent, and the problem grows, takes on a larger scale, and ends up exploding. Those who flee from problems do not know that they oxidize the emotional competence called resilience by not facing problems; they do not learn to manage and solve them. There is no greater misfortune than being lucky enough to not find problems because you will end up being close to being useless when a real problem actually occurs.

Generalization

It is quite common to hear statements with "never, ever, always, everything, nothing, people, the world..." They are resounding statements that hide a generalization mechanism; that is, a generalization is made from a fact that will always be greatly exaggerated. Generalizing is a cognitive bias. "People don't value me," "nobody takes me into account," "everyone goes their own way," "I will never achieve it," "I will always be like this," these are resounding statements that are only true in those who state that is how they see something, that is how they think, and that is how they feel, but it is not like that all. These types of statements leave one struck down, unable to react in a productive way. Perhaps, one of the most negative generalizations is "I am like this" because it means not accepting the possibility of learning, changing, and being another way. A better way or state of being.

Polarization

Some people classify or organize themselves and other people into two distinct categories or groups, "mine" and "those who are against me." This perception is absurd. People should not be distributed in this way; it is a categorization that you do in your head, leading you to perceive people in a double category. "Good and bad," "rich and poor," "right and left" are categorizations that do not respond to reality very well and are a very crude simplification. People are not one way or another; they are a bit of both; everything is more relative and nuanced. Polarization often responds to a manipulative desire to use people and confront them in order to obtain some kind of advantage or benefit.

Attend to what remains

When you evaluate yourself, look back, pay attention to the path you walked, the obstacles overcome, the lessons learned. You will perceive a lot to be proud of and satisfied with. This kind of mental evaluation is positive because it is realistic and because it gives the better more positive energy to continue moving forward. Many people refuse to value their progress, no matter how large or small the progress was, and so they look forward only to the long term, often pie-in-the-sky results. They want to change, and they are achieving it in a very respectable way, they do have many reasons to value their effort and progress, but they refuse to do so. They are still aware of the path they have yet to travel and the distance they still have to travel to reach the goal they want to experience which in the present isn't as they want it to be. This type of evaluation generates frustration, discouragement, and invites others to leave quickly.

"Irrational" thoughts

Irrational thoughts are expectations that go against logic, against reason, whose probabilities of occurring are minimal at best - expecting pears with an elm tree for instance. Irrational thoughts often generate frustration in others and self; it is, as it were, an invitation to sign up to live a disappointed life. Irrational thoughts are illogical thoughts and expectations that go against the facts' logic. Among the somewhat large array of irrational thoughts, the most widespread are the following:

- Everyone should appreciate me.
- It is terrible to make mistakes.
- It is terrible that things go wrong.
- I can't control my emotions.
- It is too difficult to achieve self-discipline.
- I can't stand how others act.
- I can't change the way I am.
- Situations that I have experienced before will always affect me.
- There is an ideal solution for every problem.
- I should do better than others.
- If others criticize me, I have made a mistake.

- I can't change my thoughts or the way I take things.
- You should always help out where you need help.
- I must never be weak.
- It is better not to expect anything from others or life so as to not be disappointed.
- Others are not as upset as I am.
- It should never hurt anyone.
- Strong people don't ask for help.
- I must hide my ignorance when I do not know something.
- I can only do things when I'm in the mood.
- It is not good to ask for favors.
- Possible is the same as probable.
- I am inferior to others.
- I am always the center of attention; I feel like I am being observed or examined.
- I don't understand why other people act or are that way.
- Giving up is the best strategy to avoid suffering.
- I must be sure before making a decision.
- One must have guarantees before acting.
- It is desirable to be on good terms with everyone.
- Change is not normal or natural.
- It is essential to know the why of everything.
- There is always something behind the behavior of others.
- People should trust me.
- You should always be excited or happy.
- I am a "jinx"; I have no "luck," it is written in "my destiny."
- Facing problems is very hard, and it hurts me a lot.

Well, you get the basic idea. If some of these apply to you and you want to change your way of thinking, then don't resign yourself to being who you are currently being. Especially if you don't like yourself as you are.

Anyone should have the aspiration to feel good and to be happy. And, people can change if they decide to work on themselves, their life, or both. Nobody is born taught on an emotional level; you can always learn and evolve to manage your own and others' emotions.

But you have to do it for yourself, gain efficiency, build and improve effective and personal relationships, and achieve a higher quality of emotional life.

You can make a better choice

When we choose a certain career or activity to partake in we are actively deciding that these things are important to us. And so, we must sufficiently consider:

- **TIME**: important decisions are not made from one day to the next. There are many things to think about and ponder. Anxiety indeed grows, but you must calm down and take a reasonable time to analyze the information we have at our disposal. Finding out other possible careers, occupations, alternative activities, etc., all take time and must be done in as efficient, organized, and systematic way as possible.
- **PERSONAL INTERESTS AND LIKES**: thinking about the more general activities that interest you the most is also a matter to think about during the deliberation that precedes the decision. Not forgetting that you are considering a future choice, and what you decide in the present will accompany you throughout your life.
- **SKILLS**: What are the activities in which you have the best abilities or performance? Although this aspect should not be decisive when choosing a particular career, you should think about it and evaluate it to know how your career plan is possibly related to your current skills and the necessary and indispensable skills you will need to develop in the future.
- **THE OBJECTIVES**: What objective do you want to achieve? This question is related to the achievements you want to experience, which will gradually give meaning to your life. Many times vocational problems appear because people are not clear about what they want to achieve in their life; they do not know their goals, their expectations regarding the lifestyle they prefer for the future. There is usually some need for long reflection in order to discover some of the answers you may need to obtain.

Remember too, that it's a good idea to be systematic and orderly when making such decisions. Here are a few suggestions that may help you along the way:

Steps to follow:

- **SEARCH AND OBTAIN RELEVANT INFORMATION**: It's up to you to seek and find information about all the careers that arouse your interest, and then determine which study route to go. It is important to find out about the subjects included in the study plan and any possible peripheral study areas you may need to acquire.
- **RAISING THE RANGE OF ALTERNATIVES**: in this second step, it is important to analyze the different alternatives. To do this, it is recommended to make a list in which the different careers (or activities) appear in order of preference. And to then search for alternatives that may interest you.
- **KNOW THE ALTERNATIVES**: It is important to talk with people who are currently studying or recently graduated. A wealth of information can be obtained by speaking with experts and professionals who are currently practicing the profession as well as those currently studying in a particular area.
- **FORMULATE THE OPTIONS IN RATIONAL AND CONSISTENT TERMS**: the optimal decision is the one that shows the most agreement between the aspects on which information has been collected and the values and beliefs of the person who decides. If all the aspects involved are not considered, the decision loses consistency, becoming weak and fragile.

Have you got what it takes to change?

There are moments in life when we stop and hold on because we don't know what to expect. We're stuck in a dead-end and don't even notice it. We suspect that it cannot go on like this, but we cannot look beyond it. There is so much pain, maybe anger and hurt, and it makes us blind and somewhat lame.

How often have I experienced exactly this myself in a wide variety of situations? I, too, held on for many years, maintained a facade, and persuaded myself that it had to be that way. I played along in the game of others and made it my game. There was a lot of internal resistance, and I felt that I wanted out of there and that something had to change. And for a long time, I didn't dare; the fear was too great: the fear of loss, the fear of what others might think of me, and the fear of myself.

You may find yourself in a similar situation, and you want to get out of there too? You feel that it is you who have to change in order to be happy. Then let's take the first steps together on your way to yourself. Read on and see for yourself, but bear in mind that we will really dig into the practical side of Eliminating The Negatives in parts two and three.

The first step on your way to yourself

Nobody can learn anything if they don't want to learn and don't believe in any way that they actually need to.

Change takes strength, love, and courage. You need love for yourself because: What you love, you value. What you value is then important to you and you fight for what is important to you. You surely know that already from many situations in your life. You stand up for others because they are important to you: your children, your partner, your friends, and so on.

From the love for yourself, the courage to change grows. Both give you the strength to keep going when the headwinds get big and when you doubt yourself. These times will come but they will not last! They come so that you can grow from them.

You may want to affirm:

I am brave, and I stand by myself. I am free in my decisions. I always make the best choice for myself.

Do not be afraid, and do not worry about the reactions of other people around you. Of course, not everyone will be enthusiastic about you or about the changes you are going to make, especially if they have to forego the luxury they are used to because you may no longer be available to them all the time. *"You have no more time for me/us," "You only think about yourself,"* and so on may become common responses from others but try to ignore them and move forward with your own life changes.

If your change goes hand in hand with greater success, people behind your back will most likely start talking about you. Sometimes there are also more direct objections, and although I won't go into them here, you probably know quite a few of them from your own past experiences.

Man judges

It is easier for most people to hold others responsible for what they do or don't like. After all, somebody has to be to blame because things don't go the way we imagined. It is always one's dissatisfaction, one's lack of love and trust that leads to the fact that someone or other makes a judgment on others. Usually, an incorrect judgment that is based on limited perceptions.

It doesn't always have to be a person who is responsible for everything. How about the weather, the season, the politics, the system, and so on. Do you recognize yourself in this? Despite all, often justified, criticism, each individual bears responsibility for everything he does and does not do. Simply put, you are or should be, responsible for everything that happens in your life.

You are not a victim unless you make yourself up to be one. Bad words, you might be thinking right now. It also took me a long time to understand that. It's the truth! The opinion of others must not become your truth! The important thing is: you do not take any risks when you stand up for yourself. You can live your dream, realize your goals, and you can be happy. All from a decision to change yourself and your life through accepting the responsibility.

The second step on your way to yourself

The second step is to get rid of the idea that you can do everything all at once, everything equally well, everything mega-successful, and at the same time please everyone. You may want others to like you so badly, even to the degree that you know just about everything about them; you know their needs; you know what they like, and so on. In other words, you know others better than you know yourself. Also, you may have always defined your own happiness and more general good feelings by the good feelings and pleasure of others. And so, you think you are only feeling good if others are feeling the same. This makes you lose sight of your own needs.

If this sounds like you then it's time to change all of that before it's too late!

The third step on your way to yourself

Invest in yourself! The quality of your relationship with yourself is just about equal to the quality of your relationship with all people and things. The way you see yourself and the way you treat yourself affects the relationship you have with your body. Your relationship with yourself also affects your relationship with your heart and your ability to feel what your heart wants and fully deserves.

Start with small steps.

Practice paying attention to yourself a little more each day. After every worrying thought, send a good, happy, positive thought. This way you eventually become a master of your own mind and thus, your body. And of course, this is all part of an ongoing cycle.

The way *back to you* is a way that never ends and ultimately, you are alone with yourself on this journey. This, or your way; can never be approached through another person. You then find your way when you stop believing in what others think and believe. I promise you, when you are ready for this great adventure, you will experience true miracles, rediscover yourself, and come to love yourself more! Changing takes love and courage, and it is a journey into your happiness that takes time.

For me, it's the most beautiful trip I've ever decided to take. The biggest compliment I got: "But you've changed." It was not meant as positively as I felt. For me, it was a sign that I am on the right track, on my way. So don't let others discourage you. Instead, let their comments and opinions spur you on to even greater levels of joy in your own life and environment, within and without.

Getting Tough On Yourself

If a particular decision is really difficult for you then there may be an error in your thinking. For instance, imagine that you are faced with a decision that you don't currently know how to make. You get a great new job offer, but your old job isn't too bad either. Should you change jobs or not?

Or, your relationship is bobbing up, down, and around: it's too bad to stay and yet too good to go. You just don't know what to do?

Maybe you're at a time in your life when thinking about having a baby must take some precedence in your life. You ask yourself: Do I really want a child - yes or no? You like your current life very much, but the window of opportunity for starting a family is getting narrower.

Or maybe you see a great apartment ad. It's your absolute dream apartment. But alas, it is in the country and you always saw yourself as a city dweller. What should you do? Does city mouse become country mouse? Or rather not?

Whatever your current circumstances, you write pros and cons lists, weigh things up as best you can, and try in various ways to discover which would be the better decision. As you try to find more options, none of them end up getting you anywhere.

What makes some decisions so difficult?

Because there are decisions in which no alternative appears to be a better option, these become difficult decisions to make.

Or the decision may have one alternative that speaks a lot and the other alternative, not so much. Decisions wherewith the best of intention and injected will, you can't figure out which is the better one to make.

In many of these circumstances, it seems that the decision isn't up to you at all. Simply because there is no option that appears to be better than the other and yells out loud enough to get noticed over other options available. In such cases, I believe that the Eliminate The Negatives process begins to shine a light on the best approach. When you focus on the negatives or cons, you are more easily able to see the positive possibilities relevant to your specific and unique desires and wishes, likes, and dislikes. When you ask which of these options is the most negative, then the most positive decision makes itself more clearly known. Then of course, when the negatives have been mostly eliminated there should really be no doubt as to which choice to make as positive choices become more visible.

Making The Shift - Moving Beyond The Negative

Positive thoughts can be one of the keys that transform your life. Do you know why? Because life is 10% what happens to us and 90% the interpretation of what happens to us. When we interpret in our favor which again is much easier when the negatives have been eliminated our 10% becomes 20% and 30%, then 50% and more. We reverse the positives and negatives and more of our life becomes more positive experiences which we can then build even greater experiences through even greater possibilities that are, or become available to us.

We interpret what happens to us with our minds and thoughts, so if your approach is positive, your life will be more positive. Your emotions will be more positive, and your attitude towards life will be much more "pushed forward" so to speak. And as suggested more positive directions open up for us after we have eliminated the negatives.

Why is it so important to have positive thoughts?

When you think negatively or let your thoughts follow one after another without putting on the brakes, it is almost as if you do not have a driver at the wheel of your own life, and because at times you are going through some dangerous roads with trepidation, you put your vehicle at risk. However, when you feed your positive thoughts, that is when you enjoy the trip, you are giving your vehicle another direction completely. You are then directing it along the roads that you want to go by choice, and so you trust the process and your vehicle. Positive thoughts. But that doesn't mean ignoring the negatives, they still need to be eliminated but we do that in a positive way and not a negative one. Sure, at times things can and will most likely get tough, but by taking on the journey to eliminate the negatives in order to experience greater things in life, eventually, the road becomes much smoother so you gain better experiences along the way and become aware of the greater possibilities available for your life.

Just remember that you are the driver of the vehicle so you can choose to focus on eliminating the negatives or focusing on the positives and move from one to the other until your life begins to turn out the way that you expect it to. As the driver, you decide to choose your vehicle, eliminating the negatives then imagining the possibilities, and then being positive to produce positive experiences.

Where do you want to go?

Having positive thoughts, bearing them in mind whilst you weigh up the pros and cons is part of every major life decision. You can choose your vehicle or you can let others do the driving, the choice is always yours. But bear in mind that this is all about taking care of yourself, taking care of your vehicle, and starting to move down more desirable roads in life, and that brings greater satisfaction to you.

What happens when the roads are not the most satisfactory?

The hardest experiences are also the ones that teach us the most and turn us into better people, wiser, stronger, and much more compassionate towards others. When we have our share of bad times, we can better understand each other and even help others with their process. For me, this is one of the greatest learning opportunities of the less satisfying roads, we gain more wisdom and refine our focus as we move along the road we have chosen to travel.

Sometimes these journeys can also act as wake-up calls. Faced with a road you do not like the look of, you can then ask yourself several questions to get the positive perspective of a particular road or journey ahead of you.

Positive thoughts questions

Some of the questions you can ask yourself to develop positive thoughts about a particular road ahead include:

- What is this experience going to give me? Or, what am I currently gaining from this experience?
- What am I currently learning or going to learn along the way?
- How can I grow in the face of adversity, when traveling down this particular road?
- How can I have another perspective on this problem or journey? What do other people think of it? How would a person who is different from you think and act? How would your idol or role model think and act? Which people will I be following and that admire?
- How can this help me in my life or my day today?

All of these questions and others you may think of may allow you to see the positive side or perspective, even what does not seem so positive at first glance; if you ask yourself a little more, I assure you that you will realize things that you did not realize before, and you will begin to see the good side of the situations that you may question and examine.

Ask these and similar questions for every area or category of your life in order to clearly see the negatives, which will then allow you to better see the positives in your life, that you can then quickly act upon to enhance that area of your life.

Why positive thinking is important

Your thoughts generate a biochemical effect in your body; this effect corresponds to your emotions.

It is scientifically proven that emotions such as joy and happiness release hormones that strengthen the immune system while others, such as fear or anger, weaken it and eventually lead to diseases.

That is why it is so important to have a positive approach in your life; it can and will save you from enormous emotional and therefore, physical discomfort.

When you generate positive emotions, you behave differently, act more positively and create more confidence in yourself and within your life. When you vibrate from trust and love, you can begin to attract people with thoughts and vibrations similar to yours, and you can then attract greater opportunities and situations that you do not attract when you're thinking is negative.

When you vibrate from fear and anger, you will attract the same type of situations and/or people. But remember, eliminating The Negatives is not a negative act or process. It is a beneficial and positive process that leads the way to the door of greater possibilities. Again, the phrase is not *"forget the negatives, accentuate the positives"*. It is instead, *"Eliminate The Negatives, accentuate the positives.* But if we first Eliminate The Negatives, then Imagine the Possibilities, we begin to choose the future of our own making. If we were to then look at the obstacles to that which we choose, we can eliminate those through our actions to experience an even better and more positive future.

How to have a positive mind

To have a positive mind, you need to train it positively. Indeed, sometimes it is not easy because we are continually bombarded with the negatives, which is another reason we should eliminate them first. Just turn on the television or talk to someone on the street; most people will tell you that things are pretty bad and there is a lot of insecurity, fear, and horrible things happening in the world. Many people say they don't watch the news, they just have the T.V on in the background which in effect is subliminally training them to think negatively and focus on bad situations and behaviors instead of eliminating them.

We recreate this negativity within the words we use, the analogies we adopt, and the experiences we have. The negative is striking to us because it touches our most basic animal instincts, such as survival and the fight or flight mechanism.

But thinking and living positively can be trained into us and yet we can still maintain our safety in order to survive. We just need to act responsibly and safely in today's modern society. It is simply a matter of redirecting our negative emotions and thoughts as and when they arise within us. You can start by calming your mind first through meditation exercises and such. It is also good to discover if you have a subconscious imprint that is blocking you from being more positive as discussed in detail within the Success Redefined book.

Having a positive mind is key to enjoying life; it generates confidence, well-being and allows you to more easily vibrate positively and so attract more of what you want.

To have a positive mind remember that the last word is always on your mind, ultimately. You decide if the things that happen to you are good or bad, you can decide to see them from another perspective, choosing another lens or other more favorable thoughts.

Start training yourself positively, saying positive words to yourself before going to bed and when you wake up. All of this will help you develop positive thoughts and positively influence your mind and life.

Moving forward

Our life cycle is marked by events of greater or lesser gravity that can affect us. However, what determines the greatest impact is the way or the attitude with which we face them.

After going through a bad situation, it is normal to hear others say things such as, "you have to move on." But how can we do it when we are filled with negativity regarding a situation or area of our life? We know we have to move forward, but it is not always easy to generate enthusiasm and take a real step forward.

The associated pain and anguish may have deep roots, and we cannot uproot ourselves as easily as we can imply it. But we must, in order to live a prosperous life.

We can't just dab the situation with a sponge and expect it to soak up all the negatives within our life or a given area or situation within our lives. Yet we must do exactly that. We need to be able to repair and transform ourselves. To create something new starting from the present moment, from all that we have lived and learned. This process can take some time, but thanks to it, we will allow ourselves to start over in the best possible way, by first Eliminating The Negatives. The next part of this book helps you to do just that within each category or area of your life, which leads the way to a more positive experience of life.

SECTION 2:

Eliminate the Negatives

NEGATIVE PART 2 INTRODUCTION

ARE YOU LOOKING FOR PASSION IN YOUR LIFE?

Do you have so many problems that you don't know what to do to improve your current situation?

Well never fear - You are absolutely in the right place, right now, and you happen to have a document before you that is going to take you on a journey of the mind, that will ultimately show you how to remove all of your problems, providing you truly want to succeed in your life. But before you start to move towards success you need to eliminate the negatives that keep you stuck, hold you back, and can block you from achieving anything at all in life.

There are really three parts to this process but here we are just going to cover the first part, as that will give you the know-how to take a massive leap forward *towards* your dreams.

But let's take a glimpse at the three parts:

STEP ONE: Eliminating the Negatives. This part of your journey is a process of finding all of the negatives that are currently holding you back or keeping you where you are right now, and then to eliminate them. An extension of this process is covered within the Freedom from Addictions mentioned at the back of this book in the Additional Books by The Author Section if you wish to take this a step further. Addictions, of course, can include addictive habits behavior, and thought patterns and isn't exclusive to alcohol, drugs, and other negative behaviors that zap your life and success.

Having mentioned that, I'm going to help you solve any negative that exists in your life right now! I will take you through the whole process in much more detail later when you come to create "**The Unwritten Book of You**". But for now, all we need to concern ourselves with is the book you now hold in your hands and the possibilities that will be affected by this current work's adherence.

If the problem or negative you currently have is a much more difficult or stubborn one, I will take you through a process and supply you with the tools to eliminate it altogether or point you in the direction that will eliminate it eventually. The point is, the addiction or problem will be eliminated by the time you complete this process so stick around. And before we move on, I want you to adopt an attitude of expectancy. Expect that your negatives, whatever they are, are going to be eliminated and they will. Don't wait until you finish the book. Instead, make up your mind right now that over the next couple of days and weeks you are going to eliminate the biggest part of your negatives whatever they are. Then do the work to accomplish that.

Know Thyself - The Starting Place is The Self. In the land of the spirit, you are always at the beginning - Oracle at Delphi.

STEP TWO: Become the Positives. This is an extension of the old *Accentuate the Positives* quote or saying. However, to become the positives isn't exactly what we are referring to here. Instead, after eliminating the negatives (Step 1), in step two we are really imagining the possibilities and the promise that the possibilities may bring. It is only by continuing the cycle of Steps 1 and 2 that any success at all can occur. It is the foundation of success if you will. A cycle that never ends and that which continually provides the solid ground to build even greater success far into the future.

STEP THREE: Create a Life You Love. This part helps you find your passion and to build a life around that passion. This third part is covered within the three main success titles named at the back of the book, and already mentioned in the preface to this present document, and in and of itself is a three-level process.

So, back to the purpose of this book which prepares the ground for the others. The process is simple and goes something like this. Think of any problem or addiction that you want to eliminate from your life and use this process to eliminate it for good. I will use a smoking addiction as a metaphor to help you understand how this method can be applied to any addiction or bad habit.

However, a word of caution.

Within this book, I will be mentioning groups or agencies and will be speaking of them in a somewhat negative way. It should be made clear right from the outset that I do not think about those agencies in a negative way at all. I am actually very grateful for their existence, both for the help and support they have given me in the past as well as the help they give to others. And so, I am using these agencies as an example only. A metaphor if you will.

I accept full responsibility for my own life on every level and seek to neither blame nor render a general scapegoat of the agencies mentioned herein, in any way whatsoever.

Note: There is a big difference between blaming the world or government, or any other agency for your problems and taking a good look at the world and changing yourself based on your findings and discoveries. This is truly taking responsibility for your own life. Having said all of that, and without further ado, let's carry on and learn these techniques that will make a warrior of you by killing the wimp within.

The Science of Affirmations.

Traditionally in affirmations, the experts say DON'T use words like NO, NOT, DON'T, etc. They do this to get you to affirm on the positive and at the same time state that affirmations should be stated on the positive. Keep everything positive they say.

For example, if you are unable to concentrate for any length of time, instead of using the affirmation "I don't lack concentration anymore". They teach you to affirm a positive statement such as: "I concentrate easily", which in most cases when affirming something that is a virtue and therefore good for you (or another person making the affirmation) that is absolutely fine.

That is okay in some circumstances such as concentration, but in other cases, you have to affirm in a forceful negative way. The so-called experts will try to convince you otherwise, but that is because it serves them in a society run by collectivism. It serves them because no person can be fully cured of negative life experiences without addressing the negatives in one's life and thereby understanding how and why the negative experience or situation occurred in the first place. I am referring here to *all* of the negatives and not just personal ones because when all said and done everything is personal to you, which in fact affects you. Remember though, that we aren't playing the blame game. If someone is negative towards you or outside influence is usurping your life and power then there is a reason that usually traces back to you.

Taking Care of The Negatives

The negatives don't just disappear whenever you decide to take a step or two in the positive direction, they are still there simmering below the threshold of consciousness, below the surface of your life. And that is the reason why some affirmations don't seem to work. They're too fluffy, too soft, too weak.

With bad, nasty, habits, and addictions you have to hammer away at the addiction from all sides. Using a smoking addiction as an example, you have to use affirmations in the positive such as I feel wonderful being free of cigarettes.

PLUS: You have to hammer away at the negative side of it too in order for the positive affirmations to take hold.

Everyone has negatives! (the addiction itself is negative i.e. working against you through thoughts or beliefs and experiences). It's just that society is built to believe that the negative does not exist, to avoid it, but in truth, it is real and cannot be avoided. It is very real. It is the sleeping giant that wakes up occasionally to take you off your path because you have never addressed it before, and so lingers in the background waiting to pounce. Whilst ever the negative exists within you as a state or habit or behavior your life will be like a roller coaster, up due to your efforts and back down due to your negatives.

To fully illustrate what I meant by the last few paragraphs I need to adopt a negative (according to the world of experts/society).

The Yin Yang of The Universe

First, let's look at Yin and Yang. Yin Yang forms the foundation of the universe which is created from atoms that carry positive, negative, and neutral charges. Now, the universe and everything in it is composed of atoms. And every atom has positive, negative, and neutral charges within and they work together harmoniously to form the foundation of **everything**.

So, no matter how hard you try, no matter how much you affirm anything, there is always a negative. There is always a *no* to your *yes*. Thinking positive constantly does little more than provide false security. A comfortable blanket to shield oneself from the real objective reality. But don't get me wrong here, being positive is absolutely essential to success just so long as you are not building your positivity atop a negative foundation. People will always be able to see the negatives within you and your life will reflect it. Even though you don't see those negatives yourself. Simply because you brushed them under the carpet of your life and your consciousness.

Affirming only positive negates the negative, i.e. you become agreeable as you strive to be and become more and more positive. Always accepting, always allowing, and never saying *no*. When in fact many situations require that you take a negative stand. And I will explain...

"*NO*" is only bad for the other party who wants you to do something that benefits them. Here's an extreme example.

If you are my business competitor and you are stealing all of my customers and in my frustration, I visited you at home and asked: "Hi, you're taking all of my customers and also all of my profits so please come with me and I will help you jump off the edge of the cliff just down the road". What would be your response? "*no*" right? Or maybe something a little stronger and dare I say, negative.

Of course, it would be *no,* and so you see, there is absolutely nothing negative about the word *no*. In this example, the *no* was negative to me, not you. It was, in fact, positive to you. I wanted you to jump off the cliff so my business would begin to thrive again so you responded negatively to my request. And so, you should. **No** (a negative) **was positive for You!** But negative for me. This is the difference between *thinking* and *being*. And vice versa?

On the other hand, only following me down the road and jumping off the cliff would be negative for you. But in this instance saying "*no*" was a positive response *from* you. From your point of view or from your perspective.

The big question is always: "No, is bad and negative, from whose perspective"?

Negativity is always negative from someone's perspective. And always positive from someone else's. This should make it clear that within every negative is a positive and vice versa, just like the Yin Yang states. The seed of one is always within the other and vice versa. Actually, the size of the seed of negativity within a positive may completely overpower the positive and of course, vice versa. Positive and negative are one and the same. They exist in the universe harmoniously together and cannot be divided or avoided.

The Negative Is Hard To Avoid

Let me give you another example. I know we need a government; they protect us from tyrants and so on. But they cannot be all positive and all good just like anything else in life. As the earlier illustration of the construction of atoms demonstrated everything in existence has a positive and negative attached to it.

Positive and Negative work in harmony together. In all attempts to separate them we fall.

Remember this? "Divided we fall". Asking you to give up the negative aspect of yourself would be like asking a soldier to go to war with a feather. It won't work out well for that soldier. You can't be all fluffy and nice, warm and good in that situation.

There has to be the opposite in everything, every time, every place, and everywhere. No matter what.

The Positive Negative!

These so-called big bad negatives show themselves in numerous ways that we ignore every day of our lives in favor of accepting a belief that everything is all fluffy and warm. We argue it out that "*No, I realize that there is bad in the world*", but we keep negating the negatives. We are using *non-sequiturs* on ourselves. We are using rationalizations on ourselves.

Here's an example of a negative argument that just happens to be true. But complaining about it is deemed negative in our society and so we never do or say anything about it. The last statement has changed somewhat over recent years but it still serves as an example of something negative being served up as a positive.

Here we go.

The subject is cigarettes. We (the smokers) think they're good and make us look good when in front of others and after sex and all the usual advertised places in our lives that supposedly make cigarette smoking a desired and virtuous habit. But that is not true. They are vastly bad for you.

They're put forward as the yang of the negative yin - and so we (the smokers) think they are good for us but in fact, they are bad for us. Now we all know this but that doesn't stop some from believing that they are getting something out of the drug. When in actual fact it is stealing their breath, destroying their insides, polluting their souls, and usurping their minds, and life.

Now back to the point.

The government (who are generally good and so we need them) allows cigarettes to be sold to the masses for profit for other businesses because they get billions in tax revenue. (doing things that are bad for you). So, the good (bad) government is making good money for doing a bad thing (allowing cigarettes to be sold and to remain a virtue (to some) within our society, allowing us to be poisoned slowly to death).

The excuse for the negative scenario is *free will.* In other words, you don't have to accept what we are trying to palm off on you as a positive value if you don't wish to, but if you will take it, we will have a lot more tax money to enjoy next year? So, we'll leave them there just in case? It sounds like a temptation trap to me!

I won't go on any further as you should clearly see that the government (who we need) is good but doing things that aren't entirely in our best interests i.e. bad. And so we begin to see how vitally important self-responsibility is.

As a short matter of fact, from the governments' point of view, Money/Revenue is more important to them than you or anyone of us are. This of course changes as the people involved in government change and we become aware of their manipulations which then makes them change so as to appear the saviors of society.

But get this... Marijuana is illegal. Why? Because they can't tax it without showing their hand. Their true colors. This is only my personal view and may not be true at all from someone else's perspective but again, this serves as an example of the intricacies of positive and negative thinking and what positive actually is anyway? Could it be as simple as being agreeable to the authorities that be?

Either way, enough said.

The moral of the story is and always is: Don't Judge a Book by Its cover, even if that cover is so enticing that it wants to take you to bed and make passionate love to you all night long.

That is akin to letting the big bad wolf swallow you all up. That would be in a bad way.

So now...

Let's continue... we are taught by the experts (?) that you should only affirm in the positive. Which is fine if you are looking for love. For example, I am worthy of love, I love myself, I attract loving people, I attract the perfect lover for me. etc.

But, and this is a massive **but**. You cannot go to the battlefield carrying only a feather. You have to take a *big gun*. And the bigger, the better.

You have to take a massive "*hell no*" with you. And that's positive, right?

So, when approaching a deceptive, conniving, manipulative, nasty enemy such as smoking... You have to attack IT, The addiction, and yourself, with the ferocity of a soldier in battle. A warrior.

You don't say (as the experts advise). I am smoke-free, I feel good and free of smoking. You have to attack that enemy.

Thus...

I have absolutely no desire to smoke.
Smoking is bad for me. I reject cigarettes.
etc...

You have to "**COMMAND**" yourself to take a negative standpoint against cigarettes and say no... Once and for all... Say No... No Freeeking Way. Complete rejection as it were.

You can then create some positive affirmations to replace the negative enemy you just slaughtered. And again, that's good. Right?

Please, if you are not getting this because of the *fluff* you have been fed for so many years then reread this whole document until you do get it.

Alcohol, cigarettes, gambling, etc... are all set-in-place systems, products, and services made to look like *value* to you but in fact, are a declaration of war against your very person, and in some cases your very soul and life. And then there's your bank account.

Your only response should be to: REMOVE THE POWER OF THE ENEMY (in your mind), And Completely Obliterate them, all of them. Altogether, once and for all. They are BAD FOR YOU. They are BAD FOR YOUR LIFE and They are BAD FOR YOUR SUCCESS. **Begin to see them as such.**

Let's move on...

What Can I Affirm - WHAT IS AN AFFIRMATION?

Well just look at the word (and I'm not going to grab a dictionary here as it's quite plain).

AFFIRM - If we *affirm* something, we basically *affirm* It "to be". Therefore, if we *affirm* it... IT (that which you are affirming) must **Already BE** for You... and I'll give you an example...

If you were a very positive person and needed just a little more positive energy to get you over the hurdles of life so to speak (but you were essentially a positive person) - In order to enhance your positive nature and energy, you would *affirm* it "to be" so to ensure that you don't slip downhill even a little. You *affirm* something that **already "is".**

Now, this is a biggy. You cannot affirm something that isn't. For example, you can't affirm, "I am a single white female", when in fact you're a colored dude. It just won't happen, no matter how hard you try.

Again, that is using rationalizations or *non-sequiturs* and so it ultimately won't work. You can become a twisted version of that but you can never be a single white female.

Obviously, you could contort yourself with outside help in order to resemble a single white female, but you could never actually be a single white female. You are what you are and so can't affirm that you are a single white female.

But to affirm anything... anything, that you are currently *not*, is an impossibility.

An affirmation is affirming or re-establishing through words or statements that you already *are*.

Here's the catch. If you are a negative (in the world's view) person and you want to be positive you can make positive affirmations all day long for the rest of your life and you will never actually be positive. You may appear to be and you may begin to act that way, a little, but you can never actually be positive by affirming it to be.

Affirming just helps, a little. - Affirmations aren't a complete solution. It simply gives you a slight state of positivity which in a lot of cases isn't enough.

My point is... that in most cases affirmations are not enough.

If you remember from the government example I gave earlier (an extreme example), them trying to get you to sacrifice your health and your life by smoking cigarettes is only the tip of the iceberg. What if that same agency (whether government or anyone outside of yourself) were to use other methods to *divide* and *weaken* you. For example, use a word (a positive word?) to describe something that was in actual fact a *command*. In life we are often forced or *commanded* to go a certain route through life, to accept certain negatives as being good and right. The same route that everyone else takes.

But what if you took control and began to question or even halt the *commands* that life was forcing on you? What if instead, you were the one giving the *commands* to yourself in order to force yourself to move in a specific direction that was more beneficial? Well, then you would actually be empowering yourself. I.E Giving *you* actual control of *yourself!*

Now back to affirmations...
You see to get the most out of "affirmations" you have to reframe them because they are not really doing much good at all, simply because if you aren't IT (what you are affirming) already, you can't affirm IT "to be" and IT will then one day become true for you. It simply won't happen. REMEMBER THIS IS JUST A PERSPECTIVE.

Instead, you have to **COMMAND** something to act in a way that is contrary to what it actually is. Including yourself. You have to be Forceful and Commanding. You have to use *force* on yourself because when all said and done, you are really commanding *change*. And not, more of the same. Affirmations in their usual context are nothing more than *fluff*, they describe something that is. i.e. I am (already) positive, I am (already) confident, etc.

And why would you want to waste your time affirming something that you already are? Well, you wouldn't. You would only use affirmations to re-affirm that you are positive, confident, etc.

Because of the duality of the universe by focusing on being positive, you would most likely bring on the opposite, but that's another story altogether.

If you want to *be* something that you are *not* already... For example, if you are negative and you want to have a more positive outlook etc. You have to use a *command* and not an affirmation. Affirmations are at best a way to remind ourselves what we are capable of being or doing.

An affirmation is a feather, A *command* is a Big Gun.

THE FIRST STEP - Before You Fall Apart

Once you are familiar with the workings of this system and understand that to promote one principle over another (it's opposite) negates the other (opposite)... this is *division,* and is nothing less than an attack on your wholeness, on your ability to say *no,* to *assert* yourself and *believe* in yourself. Then you can use it to its most positive and good effect.

As I said earlier, just like in every atom the negative constantly surrounds and is attracted to the positive and holds it in place. And that's a good thing because if that weren't so, you would sit down on any chair and would instantly fall through the chair and onto the floor, and in fact, you would fall through the floor too. Because atoms are what hold everything together. They are the substance we call matter and so if the atoms were imperfect then so would all reality and everything that exists in our universe.

Without the negative, it all falls apart. It is then just *fluff*. And the same applies on a personal, local, global, and universal scale.

More simply put, without women, none of us would exist, and without men, none of us would exist. They are attracted to and by and support each other (well they should do?). When they don't, mankind will become extinct.

A FLOOD OF NEGATIVITY IS JUST AS BAD

Of course, harmony should rule every aspect of life on all levels and that applies to you on a psychological level too.

Imagine if you will a point in a circle. A black dot surrounded by a circle. That outer circle represents your conscious mind and your link to the outside world. That is where you are focused most of the time. You are the small dot pointing outward into the world where you build health, wealth, love, relationships, etc.

Now Imagine the small dot as a sphere. It emanates energy in every direction simultaneously. Towards the outer circle and out into the world.

Now let's presume that most if not all that is being sent out are negatives, therefore other people (more positive people) are repelled by that negativity. Because they have been taught to avoid the negative and that it's bad. But, on an atomic level negative and positive are attracted? This begs questions that are beyond the scope of this document, suffice to say that everything in your life is colored by:

1. Other people's opinions and perceptions of what is good and bad. Negative is bad in their eyes and so you may repel those people.

2. Your own actions, which are also a reflection and colored by that negativity within you. Whether it's a habitual, behavioral problem, or an addiction.

So, we need to change that negative within our life to give off a more conducive positive vibe to attract positive people instead of repelling them. Of course, the law of attraction can also be used to help you achieve the things in your life that you want but again that's beyond the scope of this document and in fact, that's the second step in this process.

The answer or solution in most cases is to attack or *command* yourself like a deadly enemy and remove the negative, if indeed the negative be a stubborn one like most addictions and general bad behavior that harms yourself, others, or both. You then transform it into a positive. Make it *obedient* to you. i.e. and not serve other people (by being negative to their positive - giving them a false feeling of wholeness) or some higher good.

Actually, you don't so much transform the negative but clear it out which leaves a vacuum for you to add a more positive behavior.

Remember again that the negative is not transmutable. It is negative. It is what it is and is just a thought or belief that was adopted because of some past occurrence that caused the belief or negative thought etc. We just need to eliminate it in truth or push it aside to make room for a positive replacement. Then accentuate the positive (Part 2 of the process as mentioned in the introduction).

This is essentially how the cycle of change works. You eliminate the negative which leaves a vacuum for something more positive. You then imagine the possibilities and accentuate the positive so that it can fill the vacuum which was once negative.

It does appear like a transmutation but that is just an appearance as the negative still exists, but it doesn't exist to hinder your life. Instead, it serves the new positive. The new you. Or the changed situation. As you no doubt realize, life is continually changing, you are continually changing. The question to always ask yourself then is, what am I changing into? What, or who are you becoming?

Back to point…

So, the small black dot or sphere Is *you*, the one who sees through the outer circle of consciousness. Outward focused.

Turning inward and attacking yourself (rather than gaining mastery over yourself, your whole self) is the solution. That *you*, who has become (through past experiences and conditioning) *what* and *who* you are is working against you and your own best interests. It needs change. You need to change, to grow to transmute. That is presuming that you have negatives within your life that you want to eliminate.

Meaning your addictions, habits (bad habits?), beliefs, behaviors, values, etc. need to change. In short, whatever you see as being negative within yourself or your life and maybe currently working against you in some way.

THE BIGGER VIEW

Imagine that the black circle within the outer circle was growing and becoming even more of what it already is - EXPANDING.

Note: we are always expanding, just like the universe itself is constantly expanding, seeking more, becoming more of what it is.

Now imagine those negative beliefs (of the sphere) and habits contorting into an odd shape and no longer represents a sphere, it expands outwards and then beyond the outer circle (your consciousness) and out into the world like a big black cloud.

First, it negatively impacts your relationships with others, then your intimate relationships which causes you to lose hope and your health begins to suffer and because your health is beginning to deteriorate (EXPANDING in a *bad for you* way) you're not as fit and able to produce satisfactory results to increase your financial position, and yet your trying to succeed in life (at anything) and are always hitting a brick wall.

Well, the brick wall that you are hitting is yourself. Actually, it's an effect of your negative addictions, etc. Your beliefs and habits that are emanating out into your life, are reflected back to you and affecting it negatively (for you). They are hindering you.

So, what can you do about it?

As previously mentioned, you have to go to war on yourself and remove those negatives and then claim the positive, command it into being, affirm it to be... and then live it.

You then have new experiences based on what you send out. So...

It is true when they say.

Like Attracts Like - we must put into action new, bigger, and better causes than the negative ones we have been sending out so far in our lives. We must continue to make these changes, make these *commands* on ourselves until we have become what we want to be. To produce the effect that we want to experience.

In short - You *can* cause a new effect.

You *can* sow different and better seeds and then reap the results of a better harvest.

To reap an abundant harvest just takes a little more effort and a few more negative eliminations. And a *new way* to "Affirm the Positives". A way that you understand and that works every time.

At that point, you are just about guaranteed success. Not by the universe, but by yourself. You are the power, not cause and effect, not the universe, not the law of attraction. **YOU!** *Those are just tools you must learn to use.*

This is about giving *you* the power, *not* the universe. The universe is doing what it does and doesn't give a monkey's back end what you do. On every level and in every situation that is true. The spiritualists will argue that, but let them. In that, they create more negatives for themselves. You should care nothing about other people's beliefs. Unless of course, you do believe in those things which is fine too. Remember within one is the seed of the other and vice versa. So, nothing is really right or wrong, good or bad, positive or negative. They are just poles that we learn to live with and among. Each deserves respect as each supports the other.

WHY?

Because everyone is good and bad. No exceptions. When you see someone doing good, they are also doing bad elsewhere. The sad thing is that they don't know it. Remember NEGATING one thing doesn't eliminate it. It leaves it undone or loose, hanging around secretly influencing the good.

Best get it on your side? methinks...

Here's How.

A Final Explanation.

We make affirmations (the usual method) to our subconscious minds. We do this or have been used to doing this in the traditional way and treating the subconscious as something separate from yourself and in actual fact, it is a good idea to see it as something separate from yourself But, that can be dangerous when you think that *your* subconscious mind is linked to the universal subconscious mind.

This is the pinpoint of the negative in yin yang that ultimately links with the universal subconscious mind. Put another way, your subconscious mind is a small dot that is linked to the whole of the dark area in the yin yang symbol. That whole dark area links to the universal subconscious. And you are the head or the point within the light.

That point (small dark spot) represents your subconscious mind. and its vast reservoir of power (good or bad).

That small dot (the subconscious mind as just explained) is the small dot within a circle (your consciousness) as we described earlier. We have just put a name on it.

In other words, the earlier version of the small dot within a circle representing you and your consciousness (the outer circle) is the exact same thing as the dot that leads into the vast personal subconscious and then into the universal subconscious.

They are one and the same.

And so, when we describe the subconscious of *you* as the small dot within the outer circle - It makes it easier to describe the subconscious and conscious as separate because in actual fact they are one and the same. All explanations would then be very difficult, to say the least.

The small dot, therefore, is simply the *you* that is emanating all the beliefs it holds that are reflected in your life experience as mentioned earlier.

In other words, the subconscious (small dot) is the real you. That *you* look out through the outer circle (your consciousness) *through* "your eyes" and out Into the world.

It is at the point of " *through* your eyes" that changes can be made in your life via visualization for example but that's another book.

But as an example, if you would instead of "Looking through your eyes" outward, you could form a mental image instead that would be reflected back into the subconscious (You - or back at you) and made to stick it would then become a new belief. Or attract a certain thing or circumstance. It imprints itself on the membrane of the subconscious because it was consciously chosen and accepted. See visualize the positives. This particular section is about affirmations or *commands* and so let's get back to that.

THE PRACTICAL METHOD

So, we have seen that we must attack the negatives to make them obedient or non-affective in our lives, although they are still and always will be there - they're just transformed into being inactive. We say "*no*" to them.

Within this first part, I am going to be dealing with all of the main negative addictions, and so on. You will then receive other affirmations and commands for various positive and negative qualities if you sign up for the eliminate The Negatives workshop Program.

The actual method is quite simple, and there are two sides to it. You may also have heard about this method before but where this method comes into its own is through the second section of this book. Actually, there are three sides to the method, but that will become clear as you progress here, soon.

As an example, let's look at some stopping smoking affirmations. Traditionally, in order to stop smoking, you would be taught to read daily affirmations similar to these.

- I am smoke free.
- I am free of the smoking habit.
- I am free of the smoking habit and feel good.

Well, to begin with, they are very tame which probably accounts for the reason that they never work. They are too *fluffy*. They would be great to use *after* you had used some more potent *commands* to stop smoking but we won't make use of them here. Instead, we will rewrite them as commands. Here come the BIG GUNS!

So, when you begin to command yourself or a destructive habit into obedience your commands would go something like this:

- I have no desire to smoke.
- I refuse cigarettes.
- Cigarettes taste disgusting.
- I absolutely and totally reject cigarettes.
- I say no to cigarettes.
- I say yes to all that is good for me.
- I have no cravings for cigarettes.
- I reject nicotine.
- I have no desire or cravings for cigarettes.
- I feel good being a non-smoker.

Well, they are more demanding on the subconscious and so are more likely to overpower the subconscious mind and render it obedient to your commands.

Okay, so let's give them a little power boost - Let's add some gunpowder if you will.

- I have *absolutely* no desire to smoke.
- I totally and absolutely refuse cigarettes.
- Cigarettes taste *completely* disgusting to me.
- I absolutely and totally reject cigarettes.

- I *always* say no to cigarettes.
- I say yes to all that is good for me and *my life.*
- I have *absolutely* no *desire or* cravings for cigarettes.
- I completely and utterly reject nicotine.
- Stopping smoking is easy for me.
- I feel *fantastic* being a non-smoker.
- I am a non-smoker.

As you can see, I changed them up a little at the end and added an extra *command*. I made a few changes that came to my consciousness based on what I was reading? (effect) and added some descriptive words (green or lighter *italicized* text) to add a little more power to them.

Obviously with these *commands* being stated from the first-person point of view using "I", you can verbally or silently repeat these *commands* every morning 10 times or more, every afternoon ten times or more, and again every evening ten times or more. That should give a massive boost to your stopping smoking campaign. *(or other addiction removals).* You will begin to focus on the negative side of smoking and more easily induce a positive result of stopping smoking.

However, to really get them to work for you, you should rephrase them in the third person. Using "You" instead of "I" and "Are" instead of "Am", and "You" for "me" and so on. Like this:

- *You* have absolutely no desire to smoke.
- *You* totally and absolutely refuse cigarettes.
- Cigarettes taste completely disgusting to *you.*
- *You* absolutely and totally reject cigarettes.
- *You* always say no to cigarettes.
- *You* say yes to all that is good for *You* and *your* life.
- *You* have absolutely no desires or cravings for cigarettes.
- *You* completely and utterly reject nicotine.
- Stopping smoking is easy for *You.*
- *You* feel fantastic being a non-smoker.
- *You Are* a none smoker.

Above, I have replaced the necessary words (red/*italicized* if you have the digital version) to make the statements into *commands* that will be received. i.e. Commands Made ON/TO myself or yourself. As if from an outside source.

Speaking the verbal ("I") commands a couple of times a day is great but receiving the same commands ("You") makes them so much more powerful.

To get these commands to work for you it is necessary to record them onto a pc and make an mp3 of them so you can listen back to the recorded commands.

This video will walk you through the simple process.
www.andyraingold.com/articles/audacity-basics

After you have recorded the commands, you then need to play the mp3 or audio file quietly in the background as often as you can. Set it to repeat and have it playing in the background at all possible times. When you sleep as well as when you are awake.

If you play the mp3 whilst you sleep and as you perform your work quietly (hardly audible) then your subconscious will pick these up and you will either be able to stop smoking of your own accord or be guided to *a method or other way* for you to most easily stop smoking. Joining a stop smoking group for example and going through the process.

You will then find it much easier to stop smoking.

My own experience after creating these commands was that I discovered the information included in the next section: Visualize the positives which made what previously seemed impossible, become incredibly easy.

Lastly, the commands mentioned above reflect the decisions that you make every day regarding your addiction whatever it is. These reflect the **real** decisions you are making every single day you are choosing to smoke or take part in your other addictions.

You are choosing to accept all of these commands as true for you:

- You have a great desire to smoke.
- You totally and absolutely love cigarettes.
- Cigarettes taste completely great to you.
- You absolutely and totally accept cigarettes.
- You always say yes to cigarettes.
- You say no to all that is good for You and your life.
- You have absolutely massive desires and cravings for cigarettes.
- You completely and utterly accept nicotine.
- Stopping smoking is too difficult for You.
- You Are a smoker.
- You feel fantastic being a smoker.

Those commands and worse are what the cigarette companies have been forcing you to accept. And your subconscious supports that through your conscious acceptance of those facts and especially when you feel good doing it because the subconscious wants you to feel good so it will reproduce the craving for a cigarette. To get your subconscious to *not support* it you have to reprogram or *command* it to **NOT** support it or do something that is detrimental to your existence.

This is very true in cases where you do something contrary to your wellbeing. Most addictions and bad habits are detrimental to your benefit and future success in all areas.

The best ways to command a halt to that "bad for you" behavior is: FIRST through a decision, and SECOND through actions.

So, take action, adapt these commands to your current situation, addiction, or negative behavior patterns, create the mp3 file and start controlling your environment by controlling what you say *no* to, and subsequently get a better quality *yes!* from life.

Section Closing Notes.

To end this section of this document, if you are unable to create the mp3 as explained in the link above for whatever reason, or if your addiction is a real stubborn one you may require even more desperate methods to regain control of your life.

To that end, we have created a collection of affirmations you can begin to use in order to start removing your addictive behaviors within the Eliminate The Negatives Workshop.

We have also created and included a collection of mp3's so that you can start listening to them and begin to remove your most stubborn addictions right away.

But please understand. This method is like any other method to improve your level of success in life. They all work a little and move you to the next and best method that will work for you. By going through the process of creating these commands you consciously demonstrate to your unconscious that you are serious and will do what it takes to Eliminate the Negatives in your life. It will then more easily direct you to a method that is perfect for you at any particular time. Or, it will provide the information that you need, or will help you to eliminate The Negatives almost instantly. As in my own experience. But saying that, I cannot say that this method didn't work and the one to come did. As suggested previously, all methods work a little. It is your conscious effort and acceptance of the method that determines the degree to which a particular method works.

This method works, it works every time in either stopping your bad habit or addiction in its tracks or if your problem is stubborn, this method will guide you to the information or method you need to get rid of the problem in the fastest possible time. The command method will lead you down the road to successfully change your negative habits so watch for the signs. But not too much. This will all happen beginning the very moment you decide to write a set of affirmations and turn them into more powerful commands. And, it will begin working despite yourself.

Again, the response I received by using this method was the information in the next section of this little book - Visualize the Positives.

I wish you the very best of times and easy elimination of all that is bad for you and your life so you can more quickly begin to focus on creating and accentuating greater positives in your life.

The only question you need to ask is, "what negative addiction, habits, and behaviors are working against me in my life now?" and then take action to begin eliminating them, one at a time.

Another Important Note: When we adopt a particular self-improvement system such as affirmations or commands, it's easy to begin building up resistance after the initial period of employing the method, whatever it is. We can then take a couple of approaches after the initial period of what may seem like good fortune. We can continue using the method and build up even more resistance and doubt or we can affirm in a state of belief that what you are doing will eventually win the day for you.

Or, you may decide that the method isn't for you and then move on to the next method that may have been discovered through the use of the initial self-improvement method you used (Self-guidance).

Either way is fine but always try to do what you do, backed with a dose of belief. You will then gain the greatest possible help from the most powerful person available to you. Yourself!

Doubt whom you will, but never yourself. (your Self) - Bovee
For they can conquer who believe they can. - Vergil

Whilst I stand by what I said earlier, it's helpful to see the subconscious, higher Self, or simply, the Self… as a separate being or entity. It is still you, but not in the normal conscious awareness sense. It is the greater part of yourself that goes mostly unseen by others as well as yourself. So follow the advice of the above writers and philosophers and believe in yourself above all.

SECTION 3:

Visualize the Positives

Introduction

There is essentially a two-step process to remove or solve any problem or negative behavior, habit, or addiction. As previously mentioned in the Eliminate the Negatives Section you can't affirm something that is *not*. You must *command* It into being.

However, this will only work or, works much better when the images in your mind are congruent with the command. The whole idea of affirmations and to a lesser degree commands is to place or invoke images within the mind.

You use the commands to Eliminate the Negative and visualized images to Accentuate the Positives. But... and this is a big point... the images you visualize are negative. In the stopping smoking example, you would use the commands as already instructed. You would then imagine the command being implemented.

For instance, if the commands you used were:

- You have absolutely no desire to smoke.
- You totally and absolutely refuse cigarettes.

...then you would imagine that "You have absolutely no desire to smoke" or "You totally and absolutely refuse cigarettes". To do that you would imagine your friends or other people offering you cigarettes and you lifting your hand and saying, *"no thanks, I don't smoke"*.

Or whenever an image of a cigarette or a pack of cigarettes appeared in your mind (you could also imagine these images yourself whenever you like) you would throw the cigarette on the ground, stamp on it, and crush it. You could also picture the "Stop Smoking" sign superimposed on the cigarette, or pack of cigarettes. Any of these destructive type affirmations or images, although they are usually put across as negative, they are not. They are positive for you. Stamp on the cigarette pack, throw the cigarette on the floor and crush them. Snap the cigarette in half in your mind and you will very soon see that your life or rather your habit will begin to follow suit. But do this only after you have used the recordings of your commands to allow your subconscious self to understand what you want to achieve and to make absolutely sure your habit, whatever it is gets crushed.

If your negative is drinking, smash the bottles, throw them away, and other similar images. If your negative is gambling rip the cards up, turn over the roulette table or other similar destructive type images. Remember you are destroying a habit or addiction so you go to war and fight that enemy with destructive images.

Do You Have Trouble Visualizing?

However, it seems that most people don't have a very solid belief in their own visualizations and ability to visualize which is very understandable knowing the reasons.

The main reasons that you can't, or find it difficult to visualize are:

1. All the confusion, negative energy, and frankly, the crap left from the negatives. Negative mind-space.
2. Because you don't understand what visualizing really is because you haven't been taught what visualization is and how it works.

The only real reason that you can't visualize is that someone is telling you that you can't. An expert (not all) will suggest that "you may find images difficult to form, all you see is darkness, unclear images" etc. You respond, "Yes that is exactly how it is for me", and therefore you can't visualize. Because you accept that you can't.

The Solution I am going to present to you now is simple and you will receive the solution to your lack of visualization ability right here within these pages.

Later we will return to the stopping smoking example from the first Eliminate the Negatives section but for now, let's go a little more in-depth and continue where the previous section of this book essentially left off.

Visualization Essentials

Here we will go more in-depth with the main tool of creation, visualization. And by that, I mean to pass on a few of my own personal perspectives and theories on visualization that are not usually mentioned by most teachers of visualization methods and so you most likely will not have heard these methods before. But you will accept them to be true as we go because unconsciously you already know this to be the case. Most likely, you just aren't sufficiently consciously aware of it.

In the past, I have studied visualization and the implications but no one ever explained the subject fully. A simple but vital set of facts had been eliminated from the whole subject of visualization. Instead, most of the experts went right around the houses so to speak, to get me to form images in my mind but the *how* was never mentioned. "Just form an image in your mind. Practice and one day you will do it perfectly every time" they said. That's like saying "play that guitar" when you have never had a lesson on "how to" play the guitar. And so, it's clear at that point that you wouldn't be very capable of forming the image in your mind. Incidentally, I go into this deeper in the Success Beyond Purpose Program, but we still get a clear view of what visualization is here.

This simple secret of visualization may have passed your ears a thousand times before and its ability to help you achieve just about anything. But as previously mentioned the vital points were most likely never discussed so you only got a disintegrated concept of how it works. You are always left hanging. "Visualize your dream and it will one day come true", they say - That's it.

To go deeper into this let's carry on with the stopping smoking example from the Eliminate the Negatives Section.

Why Can't I Stop Smoking?

For an illustration: In the past, I tried to stop smoking several times until I realized the power of this secret (visualization). I used patches and determination but could not stop.

It was like running against a brick wall. I was getting nowhere.

Then in one massive moment of enlightenment, I came up with the answer and it was so simple I couldn't believe it. Please bear in mind that the contents of the Eliminate the Negatives process brought me to this second part of the puzzle.

Every time I wanted a cigarette, I would create images (in my mind) of either myself smoking or situations in which I wanted to smoke, after meals and other stuff, with a drink, etc. Or, when I was flat broke and didn't have any cigarettes, I would see a packet of cigarettes clearly in my mind, a cigarette lighter, or something else to torment me. It was then I realized that my smoking wasn't a *cause* in itself.

I deduced that you don't smoke a cigarette "therefore the effect of smoking is... you become addicted". Instead... You see images in your mind (of cigarettes), "therefore you smoke", and therefore you become addicted. And there is a big difference.

I was startled by this discovery. Reread the last paragraph to make absolutely sure you understand what I am saying.

So, every time I did see an image of a pack of cigarettes in my mind, I removed it. I denied its power. I visualized the "No Entry" sign across the pack of cigarettes. A red circle with a line across blanking out the pack of cigarettes or a single cigarette. I used the visualizations and image examples I gave earlier:

I would throw the cigarette on the ground, stamp on it, and crush it. I also pictured the "No Smoking" sign superimposed on the cigarette, or pack of cigarettes. I stamped on the cigarette pack, threw the cigarette on the floor, then crushed them under my feet, and so on.

I then went to another stop smoking meeting, (I had attended 2 previous groups and failed to stop each time) I took patches and stopped within a week and have never wanted to smoke since.

I quit as if overnight because I had removed the *cause* which wasn't an addiction but instead, it was my automatic visualization of a pack of cigarettes. You might say, "A little nugget of mind programming that had lodged itself into my subconscious, and that had stuck with me for years. Keeping me in what appeared to be an addicted state".

Please reread this page several times until you grasp the enormity of this truth. THE IMAGES CAME FIRST. Not the addiction! From this perspective, there is no such thing as addiction, just faulty or destructive mind programming that at some point in time you came to accept consciously as being "good for you" therefore the subconscious gave you more of it through images appearing in your mind of the "good thing" that was actually bad. The addictive behavior.

When I cast my mind back to when I first started smoking, I formulated images that were positive and supported the smoking habit... The *buzz* as the cigarette usurped my consciousness by making me dizzy. But it felt good, I craved that *buzz*. And smoked for another 25 years in search of that *buzz*.

The essential point is that I was continuously forming images of the benefits of smoking, associating it with sex, being cool, and so on. All I can say is "great job advertisers"

This illustration is true but, it isn't exactly true as we will see in the conclusion to this current document. But the image was the real power behind my smoking addiction no doubt about it.

The Truth About Visualization

YOUR ATOMIC POWER

Here's how to turn a weak mind into a nuclear-powered atomic powerhouse.

The real truth about visualization is that when asked to visualize and we then try, we don't always visualize at all.

Here's what I mean.

I'm now going to say something that you will most likely have read before but in the past, it was presented to you in a slightly different way. In the past, this example was given as proof that you can indeed visualize, but it was a little bit of manipulation by those so-called experts as you will shortly begin to see. Here goes:

If I asked you to visualize your kitchen, you will find it easy to visualize it pretty clearly. You will see clear mental images of your kitchen, the cooker, the cupboards, the fridge, etc. Yes?

And to further illustrate that you can visualize you will have most likely been asked before to visualize your front door. And of course, you visualized a clear image of your front door, the letterbox, the handle, the knocker, and so on. Does that ring a bell?

Well, let's get to it. Let's try it! Right now, visualize your kitchen. You will most likely see your fridge, the cooker microwave, and other aspects of your kitchen. And no doubt you saw everything very clearly and possibly in bright colors too, right?

And you can do the same thing if I asked you to visualize right now your front door. See the doorbell, the knocker, the letterbox, and other aspects including the color of your front door. And again, you most likely formed perfectly clear images of both your kitchen and your front door.

These and similar scenarios are given as proof that you can in fact visualize when previously you found it difficult to form clear mental images. This builds trust in the expert as if he got you to visualize, gave you the ability, or at least made it available to you. But it is false.

That is not visualizing at all!

If you saw clear images in your mind using the kitchen and your front door as an example and proof that you can visualize in actual fact you are not visualizing at all.

Perfect images did begin to form of your kitchen and your front door. But as I suggested, that isn't visualizing at all. And what's more...

You can also do the same with your local post office. Try it! Visualize your local post office right now and you will have a clear image of just about every aspect of your post office. You can also do the same with any area of your local community. Do it right now! visualize any place in your community that is prominent, a local school, a shop, a certain street. Walk down the road even.

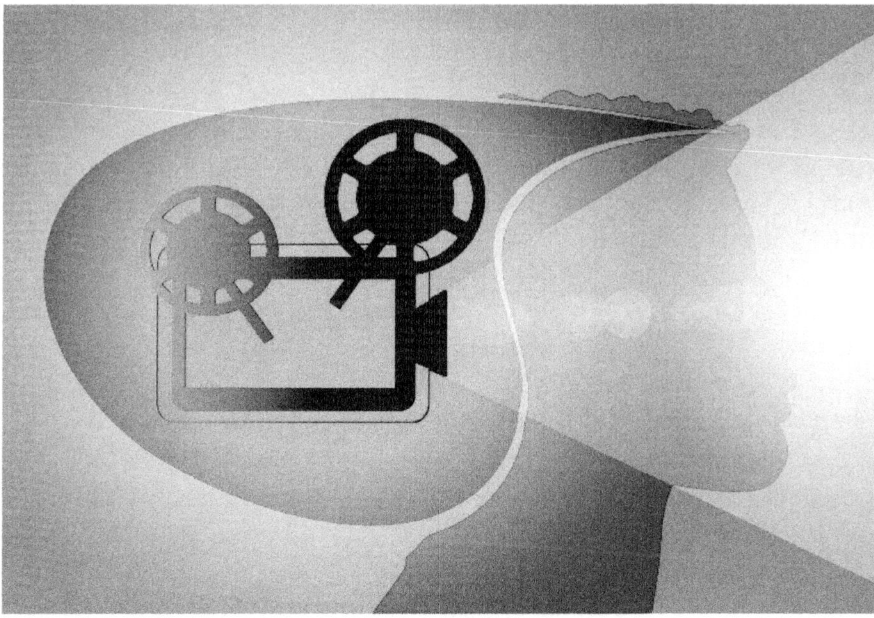

Perfect images did begin to form of your kitchen and your front door. But as I suggested, that isn't visualizing at all. And what's more...

You can also do the same with your local post office. Try it! Visualize your local post office right now and you will have a clear image of just about every aspect of your post office. You can also do the same with any area of your local community. Do it right now! visualize any place in your community that is prominent, a local school, a shop, a certain street. Walk down the road even.

In most cases, you are able to visualize perfectly well. However, as I said, you are not visualizing at all.

So, if you are not visualizing what is actually happening?

In all of those previously mentioned examples, you are actually

projecting (expanding) your consciousness into the kitchen or outside your front door, or down the road to the local post office, and so on. And therefore, seeing those things clearly and accurately in your mind. You are projecting your consciousness to that place. But you won't be able to see if Mrs. Smith down the road is just entering the post office, so why is that?

Well... Let's look at what is going on with visualizing in general and with these examples. But as we have said, visualizing isn't actually what is going on. So, what is going on in this and other visualization attempts?

When you visualize you:

- **You Project Locally.**
- **You Perceive Globally,** or what isn't immediately in your vision or line of sight. Or your environment.
- **You Visualize** what you can see with your physical eyes. What you know.

What do I mean by that? Let's take each one and explain it simply.

PROJECTIONS

When you want to visualize something within your local area or neighborhood it is so familiar to you that you can easily project your thoughts into any part of the neighborhood that you know. Incidentally, the process could be viewed as "opening up to" and allowing the post office into your consciousness after you begin to initially focus upon it. So, the image of the post office could be attracted into your mind by your initial focus upon it.

It is seen by your conscious mind as a clear and often colored image because it is so familiar. But it is still projecting out into the environment. Whether attracting or projecting true or not, the *cause* is always the initial conscious focus on the place or thing. So how you arrive at an image of the post office isn't really that important other than to understand the basic functions possible.

You can actually take a tour of your local area in your mind quite easily. Try it and see. Go to the post office, go to the local shop... walk around your village or local town, etc... see what I mean?

Visualization in this instance is, therefore, an **effect** of projecting to the place. Preceded by an initial desire or thought to do so.

But in fact, that isn't the whole story either. The reason why you project to the local post office and don't see Mrs. Smith walking in the door is that the images you project to are formed of memories of that place. The local store, post office, school, and so on. These are all memories of a particular place and so you *know* what these places look like.

PERCEPTIONS

Outside of your immediate environment - a beach in Australia for example (unless you happen to live in Australia that is) you don't project because you are not familiar with that environment. You have no memories to conjure up to form the images of that environment. You can only imagine. And so, if I asked you to visualize a beach in Australia you would no doubt search your memories for things to do with Australia and most likely come up with golden and white sand beaches, large waves with surfers surfing, great white sharks, and a number of other images *associated* (to you, and from your experience) with Australia. You may also bring up images of Australian soap operas to enable you to form an accurate image of Australian life

But in truth, you aren't really imagining anything. Only when you start to look at the associations like a surfer and white beaches etc. do you start to imagine and therefore visualize. But the actual first impression of an Australian beach would be perceived. In other words, your subconscious would put all the associations together and you would then perceive an image of an Australian beach.

The image may be colored but cloudy and not very clear, that is until you started to focus on the associations, surfers, etc. then the images would clear up a little. The subconscious grabs the associations from memory and you begin to form a clearer image.

In a perceived image *it comes to you.* You don't project *to* it. It is *invoked.* And it will seem to come from Australia or Australia on the map of the world that you have in your memory. But the perceived image will seem to come from out in the world. Outside yourself. As if it is projected *to* you. But it is invoked from memories of associations you have experienced in your life to do with Australia.

The subconscious pieces together the associations and projects them onto your inner screen. And not the conscious mind. As mentioned, the conscious image becomes clear as you begin to consciously look at the associations that the subconscious brought up.

Visualizing (seeing an image in your mind) in this instance is an *effect* of Perceiving Australia/A thing or place. The subconscious grabs the associations and projects them onto the perceived image of Australian beaches and you have a clear image. What you call a visualization.

VISUALIZE

Visualizing is, of course, the creating of a mental image (by whatever means) and so both of the examples above are indeed visualizations, of your kitchen and of a beach in Australia and so on. The point here is that visualizing is an *effect.* Not - I Repeat **NOT** a *cause.*

And that is the reason so many people find it difficult to do. They try to create an *effect* (a visualized image) **WITHOUT** creating a *cause.* That *cause* is either a projection, a perception, an invocation, a memory, an association, or a group of associations. Which are also *effects* of an initial thought or desire. What you might call the *primary cause, or thought.*

Above I stated, "You visualize what you can see with your physical eyes". And by that, I mean what is first seen. i.e. all of the above *causes* mentioned in the last paragraph are all seen or known. Maybe not with the physical eyes but the mental eyes at least. The fact remains that visualizing an image, any image is an *effect.*

And once you grasp that and integrate it into your thoughts your visualizations will be crystal clear every time. And in most cases instantly.

Why is that?

Simply because the above information acts like a software program (a belief) that once known and integrated works effortlessly within the mind. It is the tool that allows instant visualizations. Here's how it works.

Knowing the above theory, think of a cat and it is instantly brought into the forefront of your mind. And the same goes for anything that is known to you. Any object you know of or any place you have been.

With places, you haven't been you instantly pull associations from the subconscious and form a perceived image of what *that thing* would look like.

It works automatically, every time with absolutely no effort.

So, you see, struggling to form images in the mind is not at all necessary. Because with the above software loaded into your subconscious (via your conscious acceptance) you instantly have the ability to visualize.

Just like you cannot create an image on your PC until you install image-creating software. Photoshop for instance. And yes, as I wrote those words an image of a Photoshop workspace was instantly placed in my mind. That's how powerful this theory is.

You don't need to practice at all. Just reread this theory a few times until you get exactly what I am saying and then you will instantly be able to visualize clearly, and any time you want to.

A Deeper Yet Simpler Understanding

Put Another Way...

The thought comes first and not the visualization.

This is why most people find it hard to visualize. (a metaphor for the theory above).

If I tell you to think of a dog you immediately begin to search your mind. In doing so you:

1. Remove all other stimuli from the mind. FOCUS.

2. Recall an image of a dog from memory, by type, color, environment, or other location. (what is known to you of a dog). RECALL.

3. You then transform that thought into an image that is dark at first but then becomes clearer as you PROJECT it into your mind's eye, or onto the screen of your mind. FORMULATE.

4. As the dog becomes an image in your mind you can instantly recall and then project all types and colors of dogs onto the vision board within. These are the associations as mentioned in the above previous theory. But you consciously choose a white and brown Labrador for instance or a grey bulldog. You choose any details and they appear almost instantly.

This is very much like a holographic projection.

Again, most people fail to visualize because they try to form the picture instantly without first formulating the thought. The thought is what projects the image. Without thought, the image couldn't exist and is demonstrated when people say I cannot visualize. And indeed, when they declare anything that they cannot do, they cannot do it.

This is the same as a movie projector. Without the projector, the movie cannot be shown. In traditional visualization, people try to see the screen without turning on the projector - the thought.

You must first turn on the projector (formulate the thought) which then automatically transforms the thought into a picture on the screen (a visualized image in your mind).

Think of *a thing* in words, and its image appears as if by magic.

An Even Deeper Look

Imagine your mind as a circle with a small sphere, ball, or point in the center. That center is the negative (Yin) of the projected positive image (Yang).

Without acknowledging the Yin... Yang doesn't exist either.

That small central nucleus is your center and the part of your mind that formulates the thought then projects it onto the inside circumference or membrane of the outer circle which is your conscious mind, or rather an awareness, sight, vision, etc.

The subconscious is reached through the negative of the small central nucleus (the sphere or ball at the center).

We can either enter "into it" (the ball/nucleus) to reach the subconscious and universal sub-consciousness or...

We can allow it to envelope us. This is when we lose control and the habits or addictions take control of us and our lives. We *allow* them to take control. This is when the subconscious becomes master in a particular area such as smoking. Instead of claiming that mastery back, most people put up with their habits until it destroys them completely. The individual needs to claim back control by *commanding* the subconscious into *obedience* using both the recorded *commands* and the destructive visualization images *before* he or she focuses on more positive experiences.

This is all really "Eliminating the Negatives". Only then should you Accentuate the positives. But accentuating the positives is not an adequate way to put it as what really occurs is more akin to "Imagine the Possibilities". But as I just said, first the negatives have to be eliminated. And then you have to imagine the possibilities until you come to know what you really want.

What If You Still Can't Form Images

In most cases when an image isn't projected (visualized) it is because there seems to be a blockage preventing the image to appear on the membrane of the conscious mind. In actual fact, the image isn't formed because the thought part is missing. The visualizer again tries to form an image instead of forming a thought that projects the image.

And therefore, the subconscious needs to be addressed as previously mentioned within the first section, Eliminate the Negatives and expanded upon in both Success Beyond Purpose and within other books within this series and beyond.

Making A Request

On a small scale, visualizing is asking the subconscious (forming the thought) to project a full and clear image of a thing known, all associations are gathered by the subconscious which then projects those associations onto the screen of your conscious mind (the visualization or clear image). The two go together.

Conclusion

You can only visualize what is known by the conscious mind

because visualizations are in reality, memories projected by the subconscious.

So, to change your life into something better, a new home, for example, you need physical pictures and to visit the place and create the feelings and sensations associated with that place or create memories in the direction of the end goal. This is why when using the law of attraction, they specifically instruct you to know *exactly* what it is that you want, get pictures of it, and so on.

So, in visualization, we use the theories within this document to help us **REMEMBER** - A thing.

NOTE: The purpose of this little book is to help others remove anything and everything from their lives so that they can come to master their destiny and have a better life experience as a result.

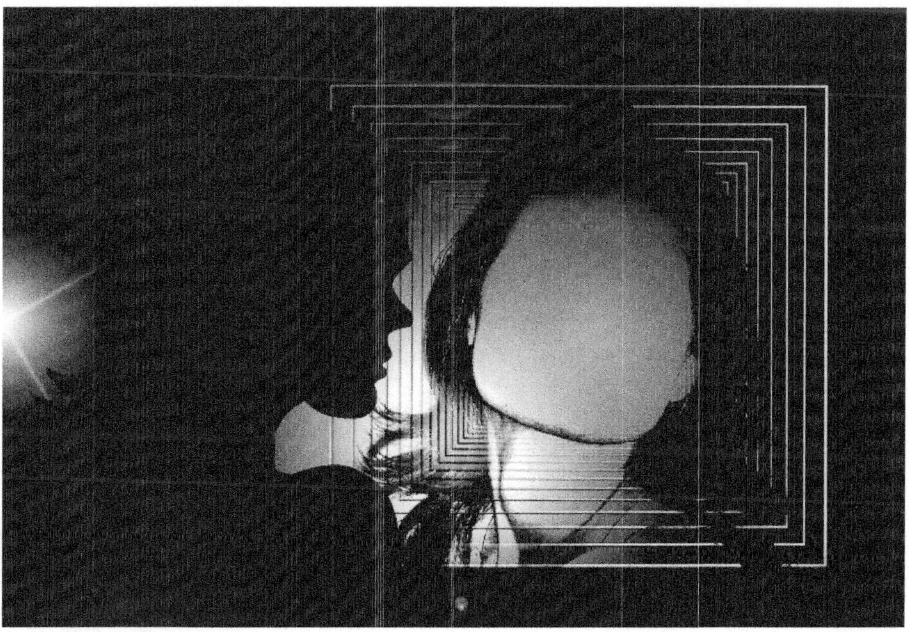

With that in mind, you may want to go right back to the beginning and get clear on what is stopping you from achieving what you want in life. To that end, I created the Eliminate the Negatives Program which takes you step-by-step through this process and includes a useful free booklet titled, "The Book of You" and other useful tools so you can start the journey to remove the negatives in your life then make way to Imagine the Possibilities open to you.

However, I do believe that the first step should be to begin eliminating some of the negatives. And you can approach this a couple of ways. You can begin to eliminate all the small ones to start, then a few of the medium-sized ones. Then reinforce some of the positives. Then complete the medium-sized negatives. You can then remove the bigger issues.

I believe the best approach is to tackle the larger issues first as these may color everything in your life as a result. If you suffer from drug addiction and the people around you are influencing your decision to use drugs then you can attack two problems at the same time. Eliminate the people around you who are influencing you and the drugs.

So, the order of the day, month, and possibly the year is to Eliminate the Negative, Imagine the Possibilities then Accentuate the Positives that you choose as an effect of imagining the possibilities and discovering what you really want in each area of your life. Then assert your dreams which of course means that you go build your house of dreams.

If you don't Eliminate the Negative before you Accentuate the Positives, you are building your dreams on a foundation of sand. – Andy Raingold

At this point, the reader would normally be provided with a list of good habits to replace the bad ones and possibly create some positive life-supporting addictions, rather pursuits. But this book is not about creating good habits - it's about making way for them and of course, I refer to this as eliminating the negatives. Whatever is working against you in your life is negative, negative, or detrimental to your personal success.

All of this elimination creates a vacuum for the new life you choose and then plan to create for yourself. This book is then all about eliminating negatives before you start refocusing on the positives.

Focusing on the positives is all dependent on *what you want* from your life which is a natural evolution of eliminating the negatives. So, this first step of eliminating the negative which incidentally, may have a few pages of plans and procedures as we have suggested.

Knowing what you want, how to get there (the goals, projects, and plans), and how to act or be (mindset and becoming) on your road, all succeed to the degree that the negatives have been eliminated. The foundation has been formed and continues to grow. Or rather, reduce and develop so to speak. Thereby becoming stronger and able to easily hold the massive structure you decide to build atop that foundation.

Based on this premise, continuing to eliminate the negatives in all corners of the individuals' life, visualizing and imagining the positives (what you want/your good outcomes), continuous study and development within the area of interests, developing and nurturing strong desires and beliefs and continued action towards what you want are the key habits everyone must cultivate. Along with developing goals, schedules, mindsets that will support and take you where you want to be in life.

And of course, good personal habits in the areas of diet and exercise, relationships and so on. I am sure you can come up with more good habits to develop.

To end, I find it incredibly helpful to imagine all of this process contained within the sphere of my life wrapped around my being and then to get that thing clean of the negatives within oneself and one's environment. Sometimes this sphere will be dark and gloomy and so the primary aim at this point is to create a golden glowing sphere, glowing in each area of your life. This state then begins to integrate with the good things you want to create within your life experience. You can discover and pursue those positive by yourself or you can use my other books to take you there.

The book you now hold your hands integrate perfectly with my other books but all continue the theme of eliminating the negatives and becoming more assertive within your sphere of influence. From that point, it's about upgrading and developing the level of happiness you experience. From here it then moves onto the three-step process to discover what you want and design a legacy, create the goals and projects that will take you there, then move confidently through all of that success.

Thanks for Listening

I wish you a better life experience.

Andy Raingold

Did You Enjoy Reading mind Your Habits?

I would like to thank you for purchasing and reading this book. I hope you enjoyed it and that it provided some value to yourself and your life.

If you enjoyed reading this book and found some benefit in it, I'd love your support and hope that you could take a moment to post an honest review. I'd love to hear from you, even if you have feedback, as it will help me in ensuring that I improve this book and others in the future.

To leave your review I have made it as easy as possible for you. Just visit or click your preferred link below.

Click Here to Leave Your Review *(United States)*
www.eliminatethenegatives.com/myh.html

Click Here to Leave Your Review *(United Kingdom)*
www.eliminatethenegatives.com/myh-uk.html

Other Books by Andy Raingold

Success Redefined
Upgrade Your Happiness
Your Assertive Life *(4 book series)*
Raise Your Motivational Power
Attitude Advantage
Eliminate The Negatives *(3 book series)*
Easily Defeat & Dump Procrastination
Freedom from Addiction
Attraction Master
Communication Master
Focused Concentration
Fast Learning Genius
Enhance Yourself and Your Life
Unlimited Energy
Set High Goals Then Reach Them
Reboot Your Metabolism
Mind Mapping Mastery Tips
Subconscious Programming
Tap into The Universe
Unleash Your Power
Creative Visualization
Your Perfect Memory
Your Unlimited Power
Strategies to Boost Productivity
How to Become an Effective Manifestor
Boost Your Self Esteem
Success Beyond Purpose - Legacy and purpose.
Success Powerfunnels - Goals and productivity.
Success Beyond Mindset - Going beyond mindset.

Free Books

First Level: Mastering Your Destiny
Second Level: Your Seven Step Goal Setting Workshop
Third Level: 5 Ways to Develop A Mindset for Success

DISCLAIMER AND TERMS OF USE AGREEMENT

The author and publisher have used their best efforts in preparing this report. The author and publisher make no representation or warranties with respect to the accuracy, applicability, fitness, or completeness of the contents of this report. The information contained in this report is strictly for educational purposes. Therefore, if you wish to apply the ideas contained in this report, you are taking full responsibility for your actions.

EVERY EFFORT HAS BEEN MADE TO ACCURATELY REPRESENT THIS PRODUCT AND Its POTENTIAL. HOWEVER, THERE IS NO GUARANTEE THAT YOU WILL IMPROVE IN ANY WAY USING THE TECHNIQUES AND IDEAS IN THESE MATERIALS. EXAMPLES IN THESE MATERIALS ARE NOT TO BE INTERPRETED AS A PROMISE OR GUARANTEE OF ANYTHING. SELF-HELP AND IMPROVEMENT POTENTIAL IS ENTIRELY DEPENDENT ON THE PERSON USING OUR PRODUCT, IDEAS, AND TECHNIQUES.

YOUR LEVEL OF IMPROVEMENT IN ATTAINING THE RESULTS CLAIMED IN OUR MATERIALS DEPENDS ON THE TIME YOU DEVOTE TO THE PROGRAM, IDEAS AND TECHNIQUES MENTIONED, KNOWLEDGE, AND VARIOUS SKILLS. SINCE THESE FACTORS DIFFER ACCORDING, TO INDIVIDUALS, WE CANNOT GUARANTEE YOUR SUCCESS OR IMPROVEMENT LEVEL. NOR ARE WE RESPONSIBLE FOR ANY OF YOUR ACTIONS.

MANY FACTORS WILL BE IMPORTANT IN DETERMINING YOUR ACTUAL RESULTS AND NO GUARANTEES ARE MADE THAT YOU WILL ACHIEVE RESULTS SIMILAR TO OURS OR ANYBODY ELSE'S, IN FACT, NO GUARANTEES ARE MADE THAT YOU WILL ACHIEVE ANY RESULTS FROM OUR IDEAS AND TECHNIQUES IN OUR MATERIAL.

The author and publisher disclaim any warranties (express or implied), merchantability, or fitness for any particular purpose. The author and publisher shall in no event be held liable to any party for any direct, indirect, punitive, special, incidental, or other consequential damages arising directly or indirectly from any use of this material, which is provided "as is", and without warranties.

As always, the advice of a competent professional should be sought.

The author and publisher do not warrant the performance, effectiveness, or applicability of any sites listed or linked to in this report. All links are for information purposes only and are not warranted for content, accuracy, or any other implied or explicit purpose.

Printed in Great Britain
by Amazon

52753156R00136